APPALACHIAN
REVIEW

VOL. 49, NO. 1
WINTER 2021

TRADITION. DIVERSITY. CHANGE.

ESTABLISHED IN 1973
PUBLISHED QUARTERLY
by Berea College
www.appalachianreview.net

©2021 by Berea College. Vol. 49, No. 1, Winter 2021. All rights reserved. No part of this publication may be reproduced without the prior permission of *Appalachian Review*. Periodicals postage paid at Berea, Kentucky, and at additional mailing offices. ISSN# 03632318.

The short stories in this publication are works of fiction. Names, characters, places, and incidents are either the products of the authors' imaginations or are used fictitiously. Any resemblance to actual events, locales, or persons, living or dead, is entirely coincidental. The views expressed in the creative nonfiction herein are solely those of the authors. Electronic submissions only at www.appalachianreview.net. Distributed through a partnership between the University of North Carolina Press and Duke University Press. Basic subscription price: $30/year for individuals, $60/year for institutions. For subscription requests and inquiries, visit the magazine's website, email subscriptions@dukeupress.edu, or call 888-651-0122 (toll-free in the US and Canada) or 919-688-5134.

CONTENTS

INTERVIEW

BOOK REVIEWS

COVER PHOTOGRAPH

Tinsel Graveyard by Greta McDonough

EDITOR'S NOTE

JASON KYLE HOWARD

Hope is the thing with feathers / That perches in the soul," Emily Dickinson famously proclaimed—words that seem to offer particular sustenance during this cruel winter. Amidst the rising numbers of cases and deaths from Covid-19, the social isolation wrought by the pandemic, as well as widespread devastation from ice, snowstorms, and flooding, it would be easy to forget what is ahead. Vaccines—the promise of protection from the virus and of safe reunions with loved ones—and always, the blooming daffodils, crocuses, dogwoods, and redbuds signaling the coming spring.

Already the trees around our house are beginning to trill with birdsong, and I can't help but connect that reminder of hope, of what's to come, with this issue of *Appalachian Review*. These pages contain a stunning debut—"The Trouble With Snakes," a short story from Monica Brashears centered on agency, with a vivid sense of place and a remarkable voice—a gripping story from Laura Demers that offers a memorable portrait of a young woman at a crossroads, and a compelling piece of flash fiction from Michael Alessi. Award-winning essayist Martha Grace Duncan contributes an aching elegy to her childhood homeplace and landscape. Our poetry showcases the glory and brutality of the natural world, the "angry din" of noise and silence, how love and desire can emerge from ruins, and an inventory of the body. In our conversation, Leah Hampton talks with Annie Frazier about *F*ckface and Other Stories*, her debut short story collection that was released last year to widespread acclaim, offering insight into her writing process and the wonder that is Dollywood.

As you pore over these pages, allow the words of these writers and Dickinson's wise observation to seep beneath your skin. And then call to mind another poetic promise, this one musical, from Gillian Welch and David Rawlings—words that I have been increasingly singing around the house: "Winter's come and gone / a little bird told me so." ∎

THE TROUBLE WITH SNAKES

MONICA BRASHEARS

I ain't got much to say but the truth. I swear by God, President Kennedy, by each of my ten toes and every Tennessean sunset—I ain't got it in me to hurt nobody. I only know that what I been doing would put my mama to tears. *You acting out,* my mama would say if she knew. She says it to me all the time. *Baby Greene, you acting out, s*he said when I threw a branch at my cousin. It was never his fault. That was fourteen years ago. We was little then. I was six. He was eleven. Josiah is his name, and Josiah is probably why I done all that I done. He's in the hospital. Rain on roads, old pickup flipped into a ravine, brain soup. Mama told me to visit him before it's too late.

Yeah, I been acting out, alright. But I ain't done no wrong, not really.

To make sense of it all, I got to go back a little. My misbehaving started the day after Josiah's accident. I went down to the colored grocer to buy some scented paraffin candles and some pralines. When Mama gets upset, she fills the house with light. When Mama gets upset, she gobbles up enough sugar to rot the teeth in her head and mine, too. I couldn't find the candles, and I was about ready to quit looking 'cause they smell like funeral flowers anyway. But I knew it'd make Mama feel better, so I figured I'd ask a worker. The first one I found smiled right away, and in that smile was clean moonlight. I put on my little girl voice when I said hello. I think it was his name tag that really got me—Otis. Don't it sound like he should be singing something to me? Then I found out his last name when we got to talking. Sweet. And yes, Lord, he was walking black sugarcane.

That night, we parked his daddy's car on the side of a mountain. He cracked the windows to let in some air. It got hot and humid in there fast. A thunderstorm boiled green on the horizon, and then it was on us, the rain and his sweat beating my face. I knew somewhere a creek was swollen from all that wet. "You like that, huh?" he asked.

"Yes," I whispered. He slid in and out, in and out, and I folded inside myself. But I could tell by that little smile on his face he didn't know that. He thought I really did like it, the way that yes came out my throat soft and easy as cottonwood seed.

"Lift your leg a little," he said. I obliged. He nestled in me a little deeper. Sweat dropped on my lips, and I licked and savored his salt. I wondered if I still had a cherry. It didn't seem to matter much to him. He groaned real loud and it didn't sound nothing like Redding. And then he was in my mouth, a fat stick of maple, but there wasn't no sugar in his sap.

He dropped me off at the bottom of the mountain, at the edge of the gravel driveway. I tried to straighten my limp in the downpour. I saw Mama in the kitchen. I peeked through the honied glow of the window and saw curls of smoke, humid pots, grease-slick catfish popping in a skillet. I paused on the porch and crossed my legs while standing. The rain pounded through my cotton blouse and chilled my spine.

I guess I do got something to say 'cause nobody likes to talk about this. When I crossed my legs, I met a real bad throb nobody warned me about in school or in scripture. And maybe I knew that throb before and didn't know it. But this time it didn't make me feel like a dirty washrag. This time it made me feel the way I feel when I catch the spirit at church, that real light fluttering when you just know there's a heaven up there. And it didn't have nothing to do with Otis, see. I stood there in all that rain and thought about his sweat. Thought about how I was sucking up all the life out that fool. And how he thought he was making me feel good, but really I felt good 'cause of me and my pretty show.

I must have stood out there longer than I realized 'cause when I went inside, Mama sat at the table. She looked too serious and too skinny in the orange glow of the slow burning candles. The house smelled like a field of burning lilies. I joined her.

"Where you been, Baby Greene?" she asked.

I spooned soup beans on my plate, some mashed potatoes all silky with butter, plopped on a cut of catfish almost as long as Otis's—

"Bible study," I said.

Mama scooted real close and wrapped her arm around me, and I wondered if she smelled the secret I could still taste. "You a good girl," she said, "but I don't like you going out in this weather. Look what happened to little Josiah." As if that man ain't a man. As if he been wearing cologne, rooster-strutting around town, taking things that ain't his, all while teething and soiling diapers.

"Yes ma'am," I said.

"We'll visit him tomorrow," she said.

"Yes ma'am."

After supper, Mama ate pralines and half a chess pie while I showered. I made the water hot as I could, 'til parts of my yellow skin flushed red. I watched those beads of water go down the hills and valleys of me, really looked at my body for what felt like the first time in my life. I thought, maybe I could

I don't got to tell you about summertime. I don't got to tell you about air so thick with humidity it licks the skin. How all the cicadas and crickets and bullfrogs jump into the same rocking rhythm.

use this more. I thought, and don't my nipples look like new pennies? So I decided to head down to the market at sunrise and get something to show off what I just discovered.

That night I dreamt of rain.

In the morning, I stuffed what little money I had in my bra and went walking. I don't got to tell you about summertime. I don't got to tell you about air so thick with humidity it licks the skin. How all the cicadas and crickets and bullfrogs jump into the same rocking rhythm. A day so hot you want to shed your clothes and lay splayed. Walking to town, I realized God made summertime for sinning. And in the green of ryegrass, in the blush of red clover and in the gold of all that buttercup that dotted the land, I knew I looked silly in my tan clothes.

I thought there wasn't much worth buying in the market downtown 'til I found a little dress that was a purple so deep it looked like crushed blueberries. I liked it most 'cause it was cheap. I bought that and slipped out into an alley behind a dumpster. It smelled like piss and mint mouthwash, but it was hidden enough for me to change. Lord, it was a tight hug. Then, I went back to market square where white people walked their poodles and ate ripe peaches. I knew I should get going within the next couple of hours to visit Josiah with Mama. The sun roasted the cobblestone and my shoulders, and it felt good, so I decided to spend the rest of my money. I bought a tube of Yardley lipstick that was a nice pastel pink. I bought baby lotion in a powder blue bottle 'cause I liked the softness of it, and men don't expect women who smell soft to suck the life out them. I bought a small bottle of peanut oil 'cause I remembered Mama needed some.

Something took over me after I bought it. I ain't ever had much meat on me, but I've always liked my collarbones, the way they reach out and offer balance to whoever I lean into. I poured a little peanut oil on my fingertips and rubbed it onto my collarbones, and sunlight clung to them. I only had a few coins left. I spent it on a bag of candy. And so I walked in my tight dress, sack of my treasures swinging from my arm, a sassafras candy stick poking out my pink pout. Smelling like a newborn. Walked, and walked, and walked 'til the sun set. Walked and walked 'til the buildings changed from big white houses with columns that looked like fondant to brick apartments all inked up with spray paint. Which is to say, I walked to the East Side.

I got hungry but wasn't ready to go home yet. I set out to use my body as it should be used. I walked a little farther and almost gave up, but then I heard the happy clacking of drunk voices and dancing piano. The noise led me to a building that looked like a house with a rusty sign that read: *Big Joe Guru's.* Before I went in, I reapplied my lipstick and peanut oil and rubbed some lotion behind my ears. Mama says to always put perfume there 'cause the body heats it up and sends the scent out. I guess I really have been given hints on how to act and behave, hints about that nice throb. Why else we want to smell edible for someone else? I promised myself I'd stay for two songs, and if I didn't see anybody worth a couple of pennies, I'd leave. I thought, *what I look like, going into a rinky-dink bar with no company, no money?* I left my bag by the door in the shadows.

I didn't have to wait that long at all. As soon as my shoe touched the floor all sticky with spilled liquor, a man had me in his arms, spinning me around. So much noise: people chatting about this and that, Nina Simone trapped in the juke box singing *Go on and eat forbidden fruit, it's good and sweet, forbidden fruit.* I didn't even get a good look at him at first. I just knew he was fat as a wild hog and smelled like onions. I laughed and laughed as he spun me in the red and blue neon glow of the place. Air fogged up with Phillies cigar smoke.

Right before the song ended, a palm gripped my wrist and pulled me from the spinning, steadied me. My savior was short, built strong as bedrock, dark, too. But of course, we was all some shade of dark in that room. I met his eyes, and he smiled and motioned me to the bar. Before I joined him, the big dancing man tapped my shoulder. That's when I noticed his jutting underbite and lazy eye. "You a snake," he said. Nina turned into The Miracles, and he started up his spinning again.

"He would've kept you spinning 'til the lights were out," the man said. I sat next to him. "I'm Turtle," he said.

I bit my lip to stop myself from asking what the hell kind of name is that. Instead, I said: "Pleasure. I'm Baby Greene."

He pushed his plate of fries to me. "That's Big Joe Guru." He nodded his head to the spinning man.

"He own this place?" I asked.

Turtle held up two fingers to the bartender. "Nah, that's the owner's son." The bartender gave us each a shot of whiskey. "He a little..." He tapped the side of his head. "But he's got the sight. Knew Kennedy would win the election, knows the snow before it comes."

I downed the shot and let the burn sit in my belly. "Why he look at me all serious and call me a snake? What do that say about my future?"

He must have liked my little girl voice, 'cause he leaned in and traced his fingertip in loops at the hem of my dress. "Maybe he knows something 'bout how you move."

Turtle's voice sounded like jazz. I giggled, plucked his shot from his hand, and swallowed. After the fifth or sixth shot, sweet piano music trickled from the jukebox. Turtle slapped his thigh, went "Mm, mm, mmm."

He grabbed my hand and took me to the dance floor. We held each other close, and his arms felt right. He smelled like pine. *If you ever change your mind about leaving, leaving me behind.* I love me some Sam Cooke, and so did Turtle, 'cause he was humming in my ear. It tickled. Then he started spinning me like Big Joe Guru: spinning, spinning, spinning across the dance floor, 'til we were out in the quiet, warm night.

I leaned down to get my bag from the ground and almost tilted. It must have rained while we danced 'cause the concrete was slick and cool. I scooped my bag and then Turtle scooped me up, and the throb was a steady drumbeat. He took me to the alley next to Big Joe Guru's. It smelled like stale grease and cardboard, but it was private enough. I could hear Otis

Redding muffled through the walls and a small stream of rainwater falling from a gutter. *These arms of mine, they are lonely.* Turtle lifted me up, pinned me against the wet wall, and then he was in me. A pressure, almost painful, and a heat that matched mine. *Lonely and feeling blue.* He moved so slow, so gentle. Not a drop of sweat. He kissed my chin like he was afraid to hurt me. He pushed my curls behind my ear. And all of a sudden, I was a little girl soaking in milky water, and Josiah was sneaking in, and he pushed my curls behind my ears 'cause that's always how he started so I don't know, I guess that's where my mind was when I slapped his face.

"You like it rough, Baby?" And that pissed me off somehow, so I dug my nails in his cheek and pulled down.

He jumped back, and I fell on bits of gravel.

"You crazy bitch." He pulled up his zipper and sauntered back into the bar.

I just laid there and listened. *These arms of mine, they are wanting, wanting to hold you.* I just laid there for I don't know how long. I finally got up and pulled the bottom of my dress down. When I went under a streetlight, I held my nails up to the direction of where the moths flocked. A little blood, dark as oil, hid underneath. I know I said I don't got it in me to hurt nobody, but the girl who did that wasn't me, not really. That was a girl I thought died when she still believed things like making wishes when you pop the yolk of a runny egg, still believed in her baby dolls coming alive at night when everybody sleep. She's still in there breathing and wanting. But she wasn't there on that bridge. That was an act of God. I'm getting ahead of myself.

I stood under that streetlight looking at my bloody nails, wondering how I could get home when the door of Big Joe Guru's opened. I looked, and from the back of him, thought it was Turtle. Maybe, I thought, I could make things right and get a ride. Maybe I could still suck the life out him. I ran all crooked on the sidewalk 'til I caught up. I grabbed his shoulder from behind, and right as he turned to face me, I realized he was a little taller.

"I thought you was somebody else." I turned in the other direction and he grabbed my wrist.

"Where you going by yourself like this at night? Where your man at?"

"I ain't got a man," I said.

We got in his truck and he drove me back home. I'm sure he told me a name, but at some point after Turtle, I realized I don't care much for the names they tell me. They either have no truth in them, like Otis Sweet, or hold too much truth, like Turtle. All slow moving. As if I got time to watch someone turn into a man. Anyway, we didn't do nothing. He drove, and we talked. He scolded me for going out by myself at night with whiskey in my system. He had a soft spot for women, being

I'm sure he told me a name, but at some point after Turtle, I realized I don't care much for the names they tell me. They either have no truth in them, like Otis Sweet, or hold too much truth, like Turtle.

raised by them, and said I was acting plumb stupid. While he went on about the dangers of being a woman, I decided to name every man I ever met. I named this one Pastor Turn-Around 'cause he liked preaching to the choir.

When we got to the edge of the gravel driveway, I said: "Thank you."

He grinned, scratched the scruff of his chin, said, "You mind if I come inside? I got to use the bathroom."

I heard something else in his voice and knew pissing wasn't on his mind. "My mama's in there. Daddy, too." Boy, that was a

15

cold lie to tell. My daddy got hit by a train when my mama was pregnant with me. He's been in heaven so long he probably owns property up there.

Pastor Turn-Around sucked his teeth. I got out, and he sped away. I rushed over to the trees that line our property and changed back into my tan clothes. I dug in the bottom of my bag and found a stick of sassafras candy, munched on that to cover the alcohol on my breath. I wiped off whatever pink lipstick survived Turtle's kissing. I started to head home but decided to pick some wildflowers. I placed them evenly in the bag to hide my dress, just in case Mama was awake and decided to search. If she saw how skimpy that dress was... I'm a grown woman, but that won't stop her from beating the hide off me. All with love, of course.

I stepped inside the house and just as I was thanking God for my mama sleeping, a lamp in the living room flickered on.

"Baby Greene, where the hell you been?" Mama leaned forward in Daddy's old recliner. "You got one time to answer me right. One time. You, leaving me to see Josiah by myself."

I stood steady. "Mama, I'm sorry."

"Sorry don't—"

"Mama, when I was at Bible study last night, they talked about two things: how Jesus went into the wilderness and how Hannah prayed for a son and promised to dedicate his life to God if He would just give her a baby. I don't know, Mama, I went out picking flowers and prayed and prayed and prayed." I lifted a flower out my bag and held it up, hoped she didn't take it as an invitation to peek in. "I prayed to God and promised Him Josiah wouldn't miss a year of Sundays at church if he'd just heal him."

Mama sobbed and sobbed. I want to tell you I felt bad for lying, but I can't honestly say that I did. She lifted her face from her bony hands, and her cheeks shined in the dimness. She said, "Oh, come here." She cried into my chest. I pretended she was crying for me, and then I was crying, too.

16

"You a good girl," Mama said. "Your praying is going to work, Baby. We'll go visit him tomorrow. Get some rest."

"Yes ma'am," I said.

When I crawled into bed, the sky was blue with dawn. I slipped into sleep, but not very long.

I dreamt of a flood. Noah wouldn't let me on the ark.

In the bright morning, Mama fried eggs and bacon. We ate breakfast in silence. When I scraped the last bit of eggs in my mouth, Mama said: "I need you to go down to the store and get some peanut oil. I told your auntie I'd fry something up. Can you believe she's having to beg the hospital for food? Sitting there with her child day and night, wasting away."

I thought of the peanut oil in my bag. I had forgotten to give it to her. "You got money, Mama?"

She slid me a couple of dollars. "Be back by two. Neighbor's going to drive us." "Yes ma'am," I said.

I brought my bag with me. I figured maybe I'd buy her an extra bottle of peanut oil, or maybe I'd buy a couple of drinks back at Big Joe Guru's. When I got far enough away from the house that I didn't think Mama could see me, I changed back into my purple dress. I didn't have to walk far. An old man in a white pickup stopped and asked if I needed a ride. Ain't that something? I been walking these roads my whole life without any help, and the minute I put on something pretty, getting around got a lot easier.

"Where to?" River asked. I named him River in my head 'cause he was red-toned and wrinkled, looked like the type of clay you find on the banks.

"East Side, thank you much," I said. I could feel my stomach turning. His truck smelled like raw meat and metal. That's when I noticed the blood on his hands. "What you been doing?"

"Been stranglin' chickens," he said. "Alright," I said. "You a farmer?" "No," he said.

"Alright," I said.

He dropped me off by the edge of the city, the line where East Knoxville melts into forest.

"Far as I can go. There's more chickens yet," he said.

I told you how I feel about summertime. I figured it'd be a while 'til there was enough people in Big Joe Guru's to have any fun, so I wandered on into the wilderness like Jesus. I found a skinny path thick with honeysuckle and walked along it. The path grew wider and went uphill. I kept on. I heard running water somewhere. Then the trees broke open like a cracked ribcage, and there was a sign that read: "Black Fox Bridge | Hogskin Creek | Est. 1910 in memory of General Something." I decided this was a good place to stop and freshen up. I sat on the edge of the bridge and dangled my legs over the creek. I baptized myself in lotion and peanut oil. Put on a thin coat of lipstick. The current below roared and rumbled in shadowed tangles, looked scary in all the light around me. I didn't care how hot I got, I decided, it would take Jesus, Himself, to get me in that water. After a few minutes passed and I realized the bridge must no longer be in use,

I found a skinny path thick with honeysuckle and walked along it. The path grew wider and went uphill. I kept on.

especially since it tapers off into an overgrown trail. I stripped out of my dress and laid down. Maybe I shouldn't have 'cause the other side of the bridge was tarred road—but who in their right mind is going to drive off into a trail? I closed my eyes and let the warm touch of sun lull me. I thought about Turtle and my disappointment with him. I thought about Otis Sweet, and how I ain't had a lay like him since. Even without me being pleased—how nice the brine of him was.

I drifted off and dreamt I was in a barn, sitting on a haybale. Chickens everywhere, screaming. I was sure River was somewhere getting ready to choke them into blackness. I tried to say, *River, where you at?* But only the scream of a rooster came out my throat. I rose, walked to the center of the barn, and there it was: my tongue hung from a rope all cured and dried with salt. I dropped to my knees and rooster hollered some more, but the blip of a police siren pulled me out of my dream. I wiped sleep from my eyes and propped the upper half of me up with my elbow. I saw the cop car throwing out lazy loops of blue and red light.

I ain't proud to say this, but the moment he stepped out his car I had an image in my head: me straddling him in the backseat, his throat in my hand, rocking back and forth and back. But that was my only thought. I never wanted to see him hurt.

He was older, maybe in his thirties or forties. I've always been bad with guessing age. How tall he was, and that sandy hair. His eyes light and wide as the cups of Virginia bluebells. He looked like white Jesus.

"Good morning, officer," I said.

"Afternoon," he said. He grinned. His teeth looked like starlight. That smile soothed me in a way I knew it shouldn't. I know how cops think about dark women. "What exactly is it you're doin'?"

"The sun felt good. I thought this road was closed." The peanut oil must have soaked in, 'cause I felt bold. I beckoned him with my finger. He obliged, sat next to me.

"You got identification, ma'am?" He asked this while looking at the gentle rise and fall of my chest.

"Officer," I said, "do it look like I got identification?" I fell into my little girl voice, which was becoming all too easy with him next to me.

"Ain't this the part where I take you to jail?"

"I think that'd make you a mean old man," I said. I squeezed the fabric of his uniform between my fingers and rubbed. "You ain't hot in this?"

He stood and pulled me up by my wrist. He kissed me, and he surprised me with a touch of tongue. I helped him get out of the uniform. We stood over water naked and drank up each other's image. He kissed me again and tucked my curls behind my ear. Tucked my curls right behind my ear like he owned me. Then he said: "It's hot ain't it?"

We both shined with sweat in the swollen heat, and I knew it'd be easy to get what I wanted. "Sure is, and why you out here?" I asked.

He started stroking himself. "Good place to sit and have lunch. This bridge has been out of service for years. When they first built this bridge, legend is—" He grew in his hand. "—kids jumped in the water so much in the summer, they started charging. Like a theme park. Like a damn rollercoaster."

I circled him and brushed my fingertips against the head while he stroked, soft as cream. "You ever jumped?"

"I could stand to get wet with you," he said.

I strolled to the other side of the bridge, sure to bounce what little meat I have, looked over my shoulder and flashed my teeth. "Running start?"

He strutted over, wrist moving in and out, in and out. He nearly growled his words: "Yes ma'am."

He pressed the meat of him against me and licked my collarbones. "On three."

"One..." The officer brushed his thumb over my nipples. "Two..." Then he stuck his thumb in my mouth, and I made sure to move my pout to his knuckle. "Three."

We ran. Our feet thumping across the old wood sounded like a foreboding knock on the door when the whole house is asleep, a knock that shouldn't be answered. My toes stopped just before it reached the edge. I think the officer must have realized I didn't jump as he fell 'cause he screamed something that was swallowed up by the water. It almost sounded like *what the hell?* I'll keep that image of him in my pocket—his big arms reaching to the sky, the white cords of the muscles in his back writhing as he dropped into the dusky water. 'Cause what happened next keeps me up at night. What happened next almost makes me feel bad about the missing posters I saw tacked up around town.

I looked down and waited for him to break the boiling surface of the water, to laugh at my fear, down there in his quick escape from the heat. I counted to four: *One Mississippi, Two...* Only the pushing rage of Hogskin Creek. I counted to ten: *Four Mississippi, Five...* I peered and peered and whatever white I saw was only the foam of the current, the foam of snake spit.

Then I heard him near the other side of the bridge. To tell you what happened next, to make sense of it at all, I got to go back a little. When I was a little girl, Mama took me to the theater, and we watched a screening of *The Wizard of Oz*. I know now it's a happy tale with a happy ending, with pigtails and friendship and magic. But then, I didn't understand. Then, I thought witches lived in tornadoes. I thought tornadoes were the most common thing. That summer, every time thunderheads rolled in, I'd cry. I'd say *Mama, we going to get sucked up.* She'd say, *We don't get tornadoes on this side of Tennessee,* and if I wouldn't shut up, she'd say *Baby Greene, you acting out.* I'd cry 'til my eyes and nose got chapped. That's what happened if I saw the clouds. If I heard the thunder, caught a glimpse of lightning, I'd get tight cramps in my belly and throw up 'til I had nothing in me but dry panic and air.

I ain't ever seen anybody have the kind of fear I had back then. Not 'til I heard that officer pop up. He sounded like a goat mid-slaughter. I rushed over to the other side, and his body was ate up with black and brown. I thought, *how the hell he moving like that?* He jerked his arm, and a cottonmouth plunked into the water. Before I could take another breath, that space of white skin was covered with another snake. Must have been twenty, thirty of them slithering all over his body, mad as hell. He must have landed in a nest. I knew I couldn't save him. I didn't want to. He moved with the frenzy I always had inside. So, I stood there on that bridge and watched him 'til I couldn't see him anymore. He either dipped down low and drowned or went beyond the bend, washed up on land.

I don't got all the answers. I only know you'll find his car on Black Fox Bridge. You'll find his bitten body somewhere around Hogskin Creek. I only know that I saw him wrestle the shape of the devil and lose. I only know I saw the water carry him farther, farther like he wasn't nothing but a hollowed bone. ■

SHE SCATTERED LOVE LIKE WILDFLOWER SEED

Swallows write their cursive names
across the sky, and the one

caught in the back of the throat
waits to say: quiet;

be still. Before the storm,
the edges of a page torn

and burned, moving
in the wind, the rose peeking

in and out of the window
waiting for us

to blossom, too. In the yard
the dandelions clone

themselves: asexual
and turned on by the speed

of passing clouds. What story
do they tell on the other side

of this glass? Would we listen
if the prophet brought news

we didn't want to hear?
Birds watch the helpless

way everything falls
to the ground.

They know a love story like this
always begins with water.

CLAY MATTHEWS

MOONLESS PASTORAL

Tonight, an empty sky. Alone
on the porch, I listen to moths

launch themselves into the porch light.
Some nights, I walk the roads

alone, let rainfall christen me.
I suck down honeysuckle

and hope the sweetness takes root.
Ivy along the fences, sky that purples

at dawn, angel white of alyssum—
the scent of someone I love,

the inked flowers blooming
from her shoulder, the sweat

of her neck. I sleep best in a bed
of daisies, in clover that leaves

my dresses stained green.
Nature trying its best to hold me,

the scent of mildew,
the sky above empty, expanding.

DESPY BOUTRIS

MELITODES

1.
Sundays like this, alone in October light,
I hold a mirror to the face of memory
to see what vapor it can leave there,
hardly roused from another image of the graveyard—
unmarked fieldstones, burial in a high place
with feet facing east for resurrection,

burial in the wildflowers bruising
with bees, what's left of the figures
wrapped in their palls, chambered
close together. It comes back to me all the time.
There seems to be a strong inclination, a folklorist says,
to believe that the natural world acknowledges the death of a person.

The moon broke out. It shone, he said, "pretty."
I could not find any dampness on the ground from the rain.
The dead crow hung over the fence—did it hold
some deeper purpose involving the color black?
A mark on the wheat, mark on alfalfa,
as any person would make with a soot-dipped hand.

2.
My mother reminded me on her last visit to Seattle
of the bee tree down in the gully—the snag
thought empty, seen colorless, but *the tree buzzed,*

she remembered, perhaps with blue orchard mason bees
there for the tense wood, forest edge, their home:
the hollow tree moved in shakes

up the hill; it rattled flats of ivy;
down at the bottom in trickle after flood
it ruffled small water, sweet in its cross.

I wish I could remember the kind of tree it was.
And my father fed me whole honeycombs
from the orchard at the foot of the mountain,

forked from the ball jar and dripping
the seep down my throat, a brim.
My baby teeth crushed the waferlike frames.

They led me under; I ate to believe
in the tone of the land I was born unto.
I almost never saw a graveyard down in a valley

and could not find a person to ask. Here I live,
a clean continent away, and spend the coins
from dead men's held-down eyes.

EMMA AYLOR

Note: This poem uses information and some found text from
James K. Crissman's *Death and Dying in Central Appalachia:
Changing Attitudes and Practices* (University of Illinois Press,
1994) and Gerald Milnes's *Signs, Cures, and Witchery: German
Appalachian Folklore* (University of Tennessee Press, 2007).

ORONYM

In a dream, I go to the hill graveyard
and sit in a red-open wound
in its center. Steam rises

from my shoulders as if from sea.
I hold nothing in my hands. Stones,
loose in their sockets, unslot

from names. Next morning,
thick fog floats us over
Portage Bay on the bridge:

no Cascades to the east, no body
beneath. Every mountain and hill
shall be made low, smoothed to a flat

of white plain—to be blanketed
and slivered this way, to river
a thread through each hole.

The bus mumbles like a boat,
under my hip-points sway of water.
Top of my head dull with its rock.

Socked-in, my family calls it, a smoke
that coats the Blue Ridge foothills
and means—in winter—rain, slopes

around us daubed to outline, then going.
Some days the air could clear
just before night came on for the long

setting of a sun we didn't see:
over an hour, whole lit; even as we cut
the porch light, the west flared a little

still, and the oak moon drew
a dashed path through our fields.
We carried the old quilts out. It grew darker.

Every mountain and hill shall be made low,
the sky's black water puckered in places by light.

EMMA AYLOR

CATTLE UPON A THOUSAND HILLS

MARTHA GRACE DUNCAN

I. Barn Burning

Wood and hay kin burn.
—William Faulkner

I was two-and-a-half years-old when I stood at the living room window with my very pregnant mother, watching our barn burn down. "I think you kind of enjoyed it," she told me later. "The neighbors came and threw snowballs at the flames."

No firefighters ventured out to save the barn or the animals lodged therein—ten cows, a horse, and a cat. Perched at the top of a hill, on a long dirt road, our farm lay twenty miles from the nearest city, in the extreme northeast corner of Pennsylvania. We were isolated at all times but especially in winter, when snow and ice left our home beyond the reach of the outside world.

Why we were living there is something of a mystery, for my parents had hardly any experience with country life. In their youth, they had flourished at Little Rock High School, then the largest high school in the country. In my mother's final year, she served as Vice President of her class, had the lead in the senior play and garnered the titles of "Most Popular," "Class Ideal," and "Everything a Girl Should Be."

My father, too, was outgoing. Despite his family's limited means, he was accepted into Little Rock's high school elite, partying with kids from a prestigious neighborhood called The Heights—close relatives of the mayor of Little Rock and governor of the state. He also received accolades at graduation, the other students voting him "Wittiest" and "Most Entertaining" in a class of five hundred.

After high school, my parents attended the University of Arkansas, where my mother earned a degree in home economics, and my father a degree in accounting followed by a law degree.

So how did we end up on a dairy farm? The story is that while employed as an accountant in New York City, my father came to believe his desk job was making him sick. He stopped going to work and languished at home all day, anchorless and weary. Upon receiving an inheritance from his grandfather's estate, he suggested to my mother that they buy land in the country and try their hand at dairy farming.

Had my mother foreseen that this move would be the first of many, perhaps she would have wondered whether the problem really lay in his job. But this time, the first time, how could she have known? Optimistic by nature and deeply in love, my mother went along with his decision.

Despite the gulf between their background and their new undertaking, both my parents were excited by the novelty of dairy farming. "Did I tell you we have ten cows," my mother wrote to her parents, "six of whom are milking—and more CREAM than we know what to do with. I've never tasted such rich milk!" My father had arisen before five that morning to install an electric milking machine; he saved ten dollars and three days' time by putting it in himself. Apparently, the neighbors and the dairy man were quite impressed. "Dick has been working *soo* hard and is so excited!" the letter concluded. "I really think this place will be beautiful in a couple of years."

I have only two memories of my own from our brief years on the farm. In the first, I am sitting on the farmhouse steps, trying to whistle a tune like my father. I blow and blow but nothing comes out. Finally, after many attempts, a clear, musical sound pierces the air, and I run to tell my mother: "I can whistle!"

In the second, there is no scene, only words—the names of five of our cows: Daisy, Pansy, Mama, Brownie, and Buttercup. "You probably named them," said Irene, our live-in babysitter of those years, when I told her this recollection. "I mean, your father was rather like a child himself." I guessed what she meant. Being so childlike, he would have understood that naming them would give me pleasure.

My father and I were constant companions, I am told, after we moved to the farm. I often rode in the Jeep with him, taking the apples to the cider mill or the milk to the cooperative in town. During one excursion in winter, on an icy road, my father lost control of the Jeep, and it cascaded down a hill. When he brought it to a stop, I turned to him and cried,

"Do it again, Daddy!" Years later, when I was an alienated teenager, my father would harken back to our early closeness. At random moments, he would look at me and exclaim, "Do it again, Daddy!"

When he wasn't going to the mill or to town, my father would work in the barn and I would run across the untraveled dirt road to spend time with him. We invented a game in which I, under the made-up name "Mrs. Marigold," would pay him a social call, and he, the host, would invite me to have tea. In a high-pitched voice, my father would ask me, "How are you today, Mrs. Marigold? Would you like to sit down? Would you care for some tea?" Giggling, I would pretend to drink from the imaginary cup he handed me.

This game, too, came to represent the strong bond between my father and me in those years. In a letter dated two and a half weeks before he died, my father wrote me, "It is a beautiful morning reminiscent of those sunny mornings when I used to work in the barn and you would 'visit' me. Elaine just came out and 'visited' me in the office and she makes a fine 'Mrs. Marigold.'"

Elaine, my father's second wife, was married to him at the time of his death, when he was only forty-seven and I was twenty-two. The night after his suicide, she called and tried to comfort me, saying, "I know you hadn't seen much of each other in recent years, but he always talked about how close you were on the farm."

Yet for all its importance in my father's recollections and in my own sense of that period, the ritual of "Mrs. Marigold" could not have lasted long. As an adult, I was shocked to learn that our barn burned a mere seven months after we moved to Pennsylvania. In my father's memory, those seven months had expanded into the whole three years of our country sojourn, or maybe those three years had been distilled into the first seven months—a golden age when he and I shared a make-believe world of social calls and tea parties, inside the weathered barn.

■ ■ ■

But what had caused the fire? I discovered the answer only years later when—as a beginning patient in psychotherapy—I started to badger my mother with questions about our past. She said the fire had started on a bitter February morning. She and my father were out in the barn, where he was trying to thaw a frozen water pipe with a blowtorch. My mother, heavy with child, begged my father not to do it because there was hay piled up all around the barn, to keep the cows warm. Furious at her interference, my father ordered her back to the house. Later that morning, the barn burned down.

The insurance company assumed that the fire had been started by faulty wiring in the electric milking machine. My parents kept their counsel about the blowtorch, a silence they justified by the enormity of their loss. The insurance only amounted to the cost of the hay they had stored, so they lost the value of the barn, about $17,000, and the $2,000 they had paid for the cattle.

On the evening of the day it happened, my mother found my father crying in the attic. She says they never really discussed what had caused the fire, because "there wasn't any point in making him feel guilty." In the following days, my father and a hired man dragged the carcasses of the cows and horse to a field to bury them. "It was *horrible* for him," my mother said. "Horrible. He loved animals so much."

And I too must have bonded with the animals. "As a toddler," my mother told me, "you could recognize the cows by their silhouettes on the distant ridge. Once we were looking toward the hill and you said, 'That's Buttercup.' You only did it once, but I think you knew them all." After living almost my whole life in cities, I marveled at that. *Silhouettes on a distant ridge.*

After my mother recounted the circumstances, I thought about my father's decision to use a blowtorch in a barn insulated with hay. Many years later, when we lived in California, he would briefly take his foot off the brake while driving down the steep driveway of our home. And while his ostensible purpose was to give us kids a thrill, he also enjoyed risk-taking.

One question bothered me: why had my father failed to save the livestock? He seemed to feel an instinctive kinship with animals, to care deeply for them. I could not imagine my father staying out of the barn had there been any hope of rescue.

An answer to my question—more comprehensive than I ever expected—arrived in the mail. A researcher at the Wayne County Historical Society, responding to my inquiry, had tracked down the *Wayne Independent*'s story about our fire. It had made the front page. From this account, I learned that my father did not hear the "bellowing of the cattle or the neighing of the horse," because he was using a large sanding machine on the floor of the farmhouse. It was only when the barking of a dog attracted his attention that "he looked out a window of his home and saw smoke pouring out the south side of the barn... Mr. Duncan ran to the barn and opened the doors. He was forced back by seething flames."

All my life, I had heard my mother allude to "the day the barn burned down," but I had never heard these details: the "bellowing of the cows, the neighing of the horse." Nor had I known that he was engulfed by the sanding machine's abrasive noise. It was striking how this scene of loud agitation differed from the tranquil quality in our old photographs—a quality that even my mother had appreciated, though she was hardly a country person. "I loved going over the hills with the dogs to get the cows," she recalled. "It was so peaceful there."

One winter, when spending Christmas with my family in Santa Barbara, I broached the topic of the barn burning again with my mother. It was early on a clear, cold morning, and she was sitting in the living room in her embroidered robe and green slippers, working a crossword puzzle in the local paper. Behind her, the draperies were open, and through the window, a ribbon of orange light glowed above the Pacific.

My stepfather had just left the room to get his cereal. Knowing that my mother disliked having her new husband subjected to talk about my father, I took advantage of his absence.

"Mom, on the day the barn burned down, did Daddy stay furious with you?"

"Oh no," she said matter-of-factly, still looking at the crossword puzzle.

"Well, was he in a frenzy?"

My mother wearily put down the newspaper and set her pencil on the table. She had grown tired of having to discuss my father every time I came home. On my previous visit, her frustration had gotten the better of her one evening and she

"I think Dad feared complacency would set in if there wasn't something a little bit dangerous, if he just had a regular job."

burst out, "Why can't we just get on with our lives? Why do we always have to dwell in the past?"

"Remember what Faulkner said," I replied. "*The past is never dead; it isn't even past.*" She ignored my comment.

At the risk of annoying her, I renewed my argument. "It seems like an unusual day. Here you are, about to give birth.

And he's rushing from one project to another, thawing pipes, sanding floors..." I moved my arms to pantomime a rushing motion.

"He wasn't in a frenzy," she said, picking up the newspaper again. "We were just trying to fix up the house."

Later that day, I drove to my sister Laurie's home to ask how she interpreted our father's behavior on the day of the fire. She had not been born when the barn burned down, but I knew that she, too, had reflected deeply on our father's character.

We talked on the redwood deck behind her house, surrounded by vines of purple bougainvillea. I slouched in a canvas chair, looking out toward the ocean, while Laurie sat on the futon opposite me, brushing her cat with long, slow strokes. Before answering, she took a deep breath, then stopped what she was doing and looked steadily into my eyes. "He was on the run all the time; he wasn't centered. I think Dad feared complacency would set in if there wasn't something a little bit dangerous, if he just had a regular job. He was preoccupied. I never saw him at peace."

■ ■ ■

After the fire, my father struggled to remain in the country. He tried raising chickens, but an epidemic killed them all. He tried working as a salesman, peddling Hoover vacuum cleaners, then hearing aids, and finally air conditioners, but none of these jobs brought in enough money to support our growing family. My mother had given birth to my sister Ann the day after the barn burned down, and two years later, she was again pregnant, this time with Laurie. At that point, my father applied for a job selling ribbon in New York and, after years of effort, abandoned his dream of country living.

II. Vanished Days

Very much, indeed, that I wished
to remember has vanished.
—Henry Rogers

It was the day before Halloween when I made my long-delayed return to the farm. I did not want to go there and had spent weeks fretting about the trip—whether I would like the place I was staying, be able to sleep, or get enough to eat. In previous years, I had made trips to our other homes—in Little Rock, New York, Saint Paul, and Santa Barbara—all in an effort to unlock the mystery of my father's early death. But my resistance to the journey felt deeper this time. After all, I did not remember the farm; did not love it the way I had loved some of our later homes and, apart from my desire to understand my father, I harbored no special inclination to return. On the morning of my trip, I spilled a bowl of cereal and milk on the carpet. In my determination to clean up before leaving, I almost missed my flight.

Six hours later, I found myself on the road to the Pennsylvania countryside with a woman named Bea and her husband Jerry. Bea was the older sister of our live-in babysitter on the farm, Irene. It had been Irene's idea for me to travel and stay with her sister, since she herself no longer lived in the country. I would have preferred a hotel and taxi, but having satisfied myself that there were none to be had, I acquiesced to her plan.

■ ■ ■

The sky was pitch black, the rain pouring down when our car pulled to a stop beside Bea and Jerry's house in Pleasant

Mount, the village closest to our farm. Because it was late, we did not dawdle over our soup and bread, eating quickly in near silence. Then Bea showed me to my room, which was small, with peeling wallpaper. It was terribly cold. As I lay in bed with a northwesterly wind forcing its way through the cracks around my window, I could not get warm despite the multitude of quilts piled on top of me. Realizing I would never fall asleep that way, I rose and rummaged through an old bureau where I found three woolen sweaters. One I lay on top of my legs. Another I buttoned over my nightgown. The third I entwined around my feet. Lying there so tightly swaddled, listening to the eerie moan of the wind, I finally fell asleep.

In the morning, Bea, Jerry, and I drove to Brown's Country Store for breakfast with Ray and Audrey Perham. Ray was a long-time resident of this area, a farmer who had moved away for a while and returned. We took a table in the restaurant that occupied one end of the country store. As soon as we had ordered, Ray turned to me. "Your Dad was doing pretty well with his herd," he said in a craggy voice. "Now this other guy from the city had twenty-nine cattle and he was lucky to send a can of milk! He *starved* his cattle." It was gratifying to hear that my father had been doing well. In later years, he had often quit jobs and seemed to lack the aptitude for earning a living.

"Back then," Ray explained, "we used to send the milk with the creamer. If the wind was right, you could hear them throw the cans on the truck. Being a nosy neighbor, I would count the cans." He also told me about the fire. "I was there," he said, "along with my brother."

Ray looked like my idea of a farmer, with a broad, Slavic, ruddy face and exceptionally large, weathered hands. I noticed the hands when he pointed at one of the old photographs I laid on the table. "And here I was," he repeated proudly, "standing on the porch roof, with pails of water to protect the house." Then he turned to me and said, "The reason the barn burned was that you had hay piled up all around cuz your herd was too small to heat the barn. Milk cows' body heat will heat up a barn pretty good. Now beef cows won't."

Impressed with this bit of expertise, I ventured to ask the question that had been on my mind ever since my mother told me how the fire started: "How foolish is it to thaw a frozen water pipe with a blow torch?"

"Thawing a water pipe with a blow torch is one of the worst ...." He caught himself. "It's not too bad; it's been known to happen."

He paused to take a sip of coffee. "By the time we got there, it was cracklin' pretty good. They go fast, once they get started, with all that hay. It's a good thing the wind wasn't blowin' toward the house."

A fit of coughing diverted his attention. "After the barn burned, my daddy offered to give you a cow and some feed cuz you didn't have much money, but your father refused."

After breakfast, Jerry drove Bea and me to the farm, with Ray riding shotgun as our guide. Traveling through the countryside, I realized how unprepared I was for the beauty of the region. My mother had said that life was hard on the farm—that I was lonely, and we were poor, and she had to can fruit until late at night. But neither she nor my father ever mentioned that the landscape was so lovely. In the rolling hills, the horizon seemed softer than amid the angular mountains of the West, and the cattle, which were everywhere, seemed to harken back to a primitive time, lending a soothing presence. Most of these cows appeared to be Holsteins, their coats black and white, in stylized patterns. But sometimes I spotted smaller cows with dainty frames and coats the color of fawn. We saw the cows up close, drinking from picturesque streams, and far away, lying or standing on hills, beneath an azure sky. From a great distance, they appeared as tiny dots, hardly recognizable unless you knew they were there.

■ ■ ■

Eventually we reached an enormous lake—silvery-blue, with a rippling surface. Bea said, "You loved this lake as a child. You and Irene had picnics here."

So this is Lake Bigelow, I thought, *and I loved it.* But when I tried to imagine myself as a child picnicking there, the image found no place in my memory. Those days had vanished. How strange and sad, I thought, that I should have lived in this region for three years and yet remember nothing.

At least I had my parents' stories, which had become my own. In fact, one of their stories involved this lake. "When I was two years old," I said, turning to face Bea, "I wandered down to the lake by myself, and a farmer named Mr. Ignatovich rescued me and took me home."

"Which Ignatovich would that have been?" Bea asked in a crisp voice. "The grandfather, the father, or the son?" After a few moments' reflection, she came up with an answer. "It must have been Ignatovich the grandfather," she said.

The asphalt road turned to dirt and sloped steadily upward. Soon I could see our house, which looked just the same as in my photographs. It was a white clapboard structure, built along classical lines, with a commanding presence on the hill. Gesturing toward the golden-green grasses, Ray showed me how much land we had owned. "All this," he said, "was yours. Down to where that deer is grazing and, on the other side of the road, to the stone wall."

I was astonished at the immensity of our farm.

"It's been parceled out and sold since then," Ray said. He called my attention to the wall. It was dry-laid, interleaved and held in place without mortar—a practice that came from the British Isles.

When we turned off the road, I noticed the grass, freshly mowed, covering the front yard. In my old photographs, our yard consisted of tall ragged weeds. The covered well I spotted in front was another innovation, but I supposed that the clothesline, or one like it, was there when we were; and probably a cat too, like the one now meandering through the grass.

A woman emerged from the farmhouse. Approaching us warily, she stopped a short distance away and took a drag on her cigarette. She was heavy-set, with luxuriant brown hair and expressive eyes set off by mascara and thick black eyeliner. *This must be Gloria,* I thought, who, with her husband Bob,

I flushed with embarrassment. I could imagine how she must see me—as an ignorant city person, oblivious of the work involved in managing a farm.

now owned the farm. I had spoken to her twice by phone, and she had said I could come, but volunteered little and seemed unfriendly. We got out of the car and, after introductions, the others went off to see the ruins of our barn, while she and I stayed behind, talking.

"We don't farm the place much anymore," Gloria said. "We raise a pig and a cow to eat, that's all. I work in a towel factory in the city."

"So this is your retreat?"

"It's not a retreat until I go to bed." Her voice was cold, almost angry, and I flushed with embarrassment. I could imagine how she must see me—as an ignorant city person, oblivious of the work involved in managing a farm. She raised her eyes to the horizon and took a long draw on her cigarette before speaking again. "It's just too much. I wish I could sell. We've been here eighteen years, and we'll never own it." The cat disappeared around the corner of the house just as a snow goose waddled into the front yard.

I couldn't think of anything consoling to say. "May I see the house?" I asked.

She led me inside, where a large television blared, and cigarette smoke permeated the air. We went upstairs, but nothing looked familiar; I had forgotten to ask my mother which room was mine.

In the front bedroom, Gloria and I sat on the bed and talked. She told me that a decade earlier, her husband was trying to unclog a corn-chopping machine with the engine still running. The engine pulled his body into the machine—all except for his head—and it was only by a miracle that he survived.

"After the accident," Gloria said, "all of Bob's insides were on the outside, and his face was white, like this sheet." She pulled back the bedspread to show me. "Blood was flowing down the road. Some neighbors thought he was dead and sent condolences." She looked at me with her dark, anguished eyes, then smoothed the spread down again and tucked it neatly under the pillow. "The day after the accident, I came home from the hospital, and a bull had gotten loose. I was chasing it. I couldn't catch it, and I just sat down in the rain and cried."

■ ■ ■

About noon the next day, back at Bea and Jerry's house, I found myself standing beside a table covered by a green-and-red tablecloth, featuring cakes, breads, and a bowl of canned peaches. Despite the hour, someone had lit the candles, and the dining room table appeared festive, suitable for the impromptu get-together Bea was hosting.

Away from the food, the house exuded the same musty smell I had noticed the night before. In a corner of the living room, a statue of the Virgin Mary loomed over a round table, while an artificial Christmas tree, complete with ornaments and lights, occupied the screened-in porch. Looking around, I remembered my days in graduate school, when I lived in a single room with little heat, grease-stained walls, and a jagged hole in the carpet.

While I mused, a man with a gaunt face tapped gently on my shoulder. He introduced himself as Ray's older brother, Gomer. "I still have the wonderful Christmas cards your father made," he said. "Have you seen them?"

I nodded. Our family had saved and admired them over the years.

"Your father used trick photography," Gomer continued, "to make it look like you all were standing on each other's shoulders to decorate the tree."

Meanwhile, a kind-looking woman had come up to us, waiting patiently to speak. "You must have known Rufus Scott," she said. I shook my head. "He had the farm next to yours," she went on, "and cut some of your hay. One Sunday, he was in his new tractor, going up a hill to spread manure. The tractor turned over on him and killed him." Her face took on a look of deep sadness. "He had planned to take his mother to church that morning."

One of the men interrupted in a loud, gruff voice. "In World War II, Rufus transported supplies on the Burma Road." He looked at me intently, perhaps wondering whether I knew the historical reference. "Out there, he was on many a hill—one-thousand-foot drops. Rufus used to say that if a truck broke down and was blocking all the others, sometimes they would push it over the cliff."

I had not yet recovered from this tale when Bea introduced me to one of the younger men at the party. He was deaf and,

I gathered, had recently lost his wife. Taking me aside in the kitchen, Bea explained, "One day in winter, her car stalled at the top of a hill. Her brother-in-law owned a tow truck, so she called him for help, and when she was hooking up her car, the truck slid backwards on the hill, crushing her between the vehicles."

"How awful," I murmured. I was thinking of the hills; they were lovely but treacherous, reminding me of Yeats's phrase, "A terrible beauty."

■ ■ ■

Early the next morning, I boarded a flight back to Atlanta. The man seated next to me was reading a gorgeous book, leather-bound in red and gold. I didn't recognize the script. "May I ask what language that is?"

"Persian."

"Oh."

Wanting to reciprocate, I said, "I'm just returning from the country," and held up a photograph of our farmhouse, with its clapboard structure badly in need of paint and its raggedy weeds out front.

"It's paradigmatic!" he said, returning to his book. And it struck me how quickly I had landed back in my ordinary world, with its well-traveled people and exotic languages—as if by a mere click of my ruby slippers, I had left the remote place where I had been, only a few hours before.

Gazing out the window, I asked myself what I had learned from my reluctant pilgrimage. I had hoped to have an experience that—like Proust's taste of the tea-soaked madeleine—would call up a whole realm of memories. But no such experience occurred. No fluted "plump little cakes"—not the lake, nor even the house, had returned to me my lost past.

III. Vestiges

*Vestige: A visible trace, evidence, or sign of
something that once existed but exists or appears no more.*
—American Heritage Dictionary

It was early spring when I made my second journey back
to the farm. This time I had come at the invitation of Gloria,
who called me the day after my previous visit, inviting me to
stay with her. "You can sit on the porch and write," she said.

Though moved by her generosity, I was reluctant to accept.
On my first visit, Gloria had seemed unhappy and volatile.
I worried about sharing a space with her and Bob, lacking
privacy and independence. But at last, my lingering curiosity
overcame my anxious nature, and I decided to return.

At the farm, the trees were still quite bare, their leaves just
beginning to bud, but the ground below, which in autumn had
been covered with dead leaves, was now vibrant. Periwinkle
wildflowers bloomed in the ditches, while purplish thistles
and golden locusts covered the meadow. Among them were
milkweed pods that had split open, revealing tufts of white
down. Across the road from our house, near the foundation of
our burned-down barn, grew raspberry bushes, fragile white
Mayflowers, and Johnny-jump-ups of a violet blue.

Gloria too had changed. She seemed more relaxed than in
the fall and treated me with generosity and grace, even going
so far as to put me up in her own bedroom for the duration
of my stay. When I arrived, she showed me to my room right
away, explaining how to work the bed, which went up and
down with the push of a button, and pointing out twelve
Barbie dolls stacked in their original boxes like a pyramid
in a glass case. In the center was her favorite: "Angel of Joy,"
a blonde beauty with golden wings, wearing a shimmering

sea-foam skirt and a white bodice adorned with a rose. A few minutes earlier, walking through the living room, I had glimpsed another collection of Barbies. There were twenty-five in all.

"Why do you keep them?" I asked.

"I adore any Barbie with a gown," she said. "I don't open them; they're for show. I hope when my kids are grown up, they will know not to open them, and their kids will sell them and have some money."

Her husband, Bob, bought the Barbies for her. He was rail-thin and abnormally straight, due to his accident. I didn't see him much, for he kept different hours from Gloria and me, eating by himself and staying up all night to watch television. He had a sardonic sense of humor and, when we did cross paths, greeted me with provocative remarks such as, "Your team lost!" or "I called out to wake you at 4:00 o'clock this morning, but you didn't wake up. I thought you wanted to get up then!"

We went downstairs, where Gloria introduced me to her two daughters, one twelve, the other twenty-two. Like their mother, they were stocky and pretty, with sleek, dark hair and eloquent eyes. The older one lived in town with her three-year-old son, and the younger one often stayed with them. I asked Gloria whether her whole family lived in the area. "Yes," she said, "And Bob's does too. You can see his entire family just by walking around one block."

"Have you ever flown in an airplane?" I asked.

"No, and I never will," she said, pouring me a glass of juice in the kitchen. "I'm afraid the plane could fall." Her daughters felt the same way, she added, as if their feelings lent authority to her point of view.

"How do you go anywhere then?"

"I don't. I've never been anywhere."

That afternoon, she offered to show me the area. We decided to visit Carbondale, the nearest city, where both my sisters had been born. I learned a lot from the outing; it was one of the few times I had been amazed at an absence. There was, simply, nothing between the farm and that city more than thirty minutes away.

On returning from our excursion, Gloria gave me a present: a kitchen towel with beige, mauve, and cream-colored checks. She had made it at the factory where she worked alongside four other women. All day, she ran a sewing machine, hemming towels and affixing labels that read:

J. C. Penney
Home Collection
Carefully Woven in U.S.A.

The rough towel softened my heart, and I thanked her warmly, admiring her workmanship.

We went outside, where she pointed out the Canada goose she had adopted. It was penned up in the back yard, along with the snow goose I remembered seeing in the fall, waddling freely. I commented on their confinement, and Gloria explained, "If I leave it go, a fox is gonna get it. I can't leave them run free." Besides the goose, she had a new calf they were raising for beef. Like her other animals, the calf had no name, and she let me name it *Duncan* as a vestige of my visit.

■ ■ ■

Late that evening, Gloria and I sat in the kitchen eating a mixture of vanilla ice cream and sherbet called "Orange Swirl." It was familiar to me from the orange Creamsicles of my childhood, but I had not tasted that sweet tartness in many years and was surprised to find it so delectable. As we dipped our spoons into our bowls, Gloria said, "When Bob and I got married, we expected to be happy together. If we had known how things would turn out, I don't know whether we would have done it."

"You wouldn't have married Bob if you had known?"

But my shock was too apparent. "Oh yes," she said quickly, "because he was the man I fell in love with. But our lives have been miserable since his accident." Two weeks earlier, Bob was speaking of suicide, she confided, because his life was so empty. Now he was taking medicine, and his mood was better. Touched that she had trusted me with such a personal story, I felt my resistance to the country melting away like the ice cream at the edge of my bowl.

■ ■ ■

Upon waking the next morning, I rose quickly and opened the window to see the view. Leaning out, I looked down the gently winding dirt road to Lake Bigelow. A forest flanked the scene, and the trees grew so thick they seemed to be framing a picture of the road and the lake between them. Sounds of honking drew my gaze upward. Wild geese were flying in an immense sky, but they held my interest for only a moment; I was mesmerized by the road and the lake.

As I gazed, a scene came to me, unbidden, from a Spanish play. The main character, a life-long prisoner in a cave, has just awakened to happy thoughts of the day before, when he was allowed a brief period in freedom; however, as he reminisces, a guard interrupts him, telling the prisoner that what he takes for memories are just a dream. Sad and confused, the prisoner believes that the guard may be right; perhaps the events he remembers did not happen. But then he recalls a beautiful lady from the day before—recalls her so vividly that he says, "And that was true, I believe, for everything else has ended, and she alone remains."

So also, I thought, the view of the road leading to the lake must be a true evocation of my past, not something I had only heard about or seen in a photograph—we had no photographs of this scene—nor a memory that my mind had transformed through the years. It was, I believed, a direct connection to the little girl I once was.

■ ■ ■

The day after returning to Atlanta, I went to the closet and dug up my boxes of childhood memorabilia, organized by place. In my Saint Paul box, I found a stapled booklet I had made in third grade entitled "What I Hope My Future Will Be." Printed in purple crayon, it detailed the twenty-four children I would have ("Twelve boys and twelve girls. They will be twins."), the colonial house I planned to live in, the ice-skating rink, and the theater ("where the children can put on plays and shows and have circuses too"). It went on to describe the bedrooms I wished for, with their matching bedspreads, and the kitchen, with its blue counters and GE refrigerator. In the midst of all these wishes, only one was couched in the negative: "We will not live on a farm."

That part, at least, had come true. Since college, I had lived only in large cities, and now resided in a dense commercial district of Atlanta—in an apartment on the twenty-first floor, around the corner from a bookstore, a theater, and numerous restaurants.

I suggested to a friend that my love of cities came from living on a farm. "Yes," he answered, "and I don't think it's a defensive love. I think cities were a discovery for you: 'The world has more to it than the farm.'"

■ ■ ■

Spring turned to summer, and with summer came the end of the academic year. In the cavernous building where I worked, my colleagues spoke enthusiastically about the summer peacefulness, which allowed more time for research and writing. But I found the quietude painful. As a guest in my mother or sister's home, I always wrote in a collective space, with music, noise, and confusion around me. In a quiet study or bedroom, I felt too anxious and alone. I wondered whether my need for constant stimulation stemmed from the traumatic "too littleness" of my years on the farm.

And yet my desire to be with people had not translated into a willingness to have them close. In an old album, I discovered a photograph taken in the suburb of New York City where we settled after leaving Pennsylvania. In this black-and-white picture of my first-grade class, I spotted myself in a dark dress and light-colored cardigan, on one end of the back row. Standing about a foot away from the nearest child, I appear the most solitary of anyone in the class.

Inspired by the picture, I picked up my report card from first grade, printed on orange cardboard. It was my father who had signed it, in his elegant script: "Richard F. Duncan, Jr."

The report card had two categories: "Basic Skills and Knowledge" and "School Living." Under the first heading, my teacher detailed my achievements, while under the second, she repeatedly expressed concern about my "reserve." Despite noting some improvement, she concluded one comment by saying, "For the most part Martha continues to work and play by herself, except when on the playground." I repeated the words, struck by them for the first time: "Work *and play* by herself." This teacher had noticed, early on, a quality that would color my whole life—that perhaps explained why I never married or had those twenty-four children, and why a colleague criticized me at the tenure vote for my aloofness and detachment.

Worried by these reflections, I sought out reassurance by calling Irene. "Do you think our isolation was a bad thing when we lived on the farm? Was it damaging?"

She took a deep breath before answering. "I think it was hard for you. When I got off the bus, you would be waiting for me at the top of the hill." After a moment's reflection, she said, "But it's an asset to be able to play by yourself. My children complained of boredom when no one was around. You knew you could talk to the cat or the dog." *What cold comfort, I thought at first. Were the cat and dog adequate substitutes for human friends?* Then I recalled that isolated prisoners, deprived of contact with the outside world, find solace in nonhuman visitors to their cells—roaches, spiders, and birds.

■ ■ ■

During the following months, I could not desist from puzzling over the farm and how it affected us. One evening, glancing through a brochure from the Chamber of Commerce in Northeast Pennsylvania, I came across a description of the region where our farm was located. The description used the phrase "Valley of the Endless Mountains"—a phrase that sounded familiar, though I couldn't identify it at first. Then it came to me. The words "endless mountains" resonated with a favorite blessing, one I had learned in Saint Paul—three years and three moves after our time in Pennsylvania.

From the age of eight, I had sung in the children's choir at the House of Hope Church. Dressed in black cassocks, white surplices, and purple velvet bows, we children would march into the sanctuary to join the adult and high school choirs. I felt elated during our performance of the soaring music but grew bored during the offertory, when ushers, with agonizing slowness, passed silver plates down the rows of congregants. Waiting for the offertory to end, we kids played tick-tack-toe on the church bulletins, bending our heads like co-conspirators behind the backs of the mahogany pews.

Finally, at a signal from the organist, the ushers would bring the collection forward as the congregation rose to sing: "Praise God from whom all blessings flow. Praise Him all creatures here below...." Then the minister pronounced the blessing:

Silver and gold are thine, Oh Lord,
The cattle upon a thousand hills.
All that we have comes from thee.
We give thee but thine own.

As a child, I would not have known that the word "cattle" once meant all property, or that "hills" originally encompassed mountains too; nevertheless, the lyrical stanza held me in its spell, and I recited it to myself even after we moved away and went to that church no more.

Surely my attachment to the blessing had originated in the landscape of my childhood. I recalled the cattle on my recent trips to Pleasant Mount. I must have seen those cows at a distance whenever I rode in the Jeep with my father, and up close, when we played "Mrs. Marigold" in the barn. Having named our cows, perhaps I had loved them. Perhaps they had loved me. *Could* cows love people? I didn't know.

But what I did know—what I understood then for the first time—was that my years on the dairy farm had left enduring traces, fostering my inclination to solitude and my lifelong bond with my father. Those cows were pieces of a puzzle I couldn't solve, part of a formative setting that haunted me, now lost to remembrance. ∎

THE HUNTER'S AFTERLIFE

Ten bags of decoys nest in the basement;
twelve rubber waders, like half-torsos, hang
from the ceiling; shotguns fill two steel safes;
there's a duck call for every breed he knows.
His pile of possessions constantly grows
like sandbags to hold back the rising flood.

Bury him with one of each, a pharaoh
crossing to a happy hunting ground, heaven
of frigid dawns, duck blinds, deer stands at dusk,
where animals come to him without fear
when he speaks the language he knows by heart,
his rubber-coated waders grow webbed, wings

spring from his sloped shoulders, or antlers sprout
from his skull. Forgiven, he has no need of things
to run with the herd or fly with the flock,
and when the sun sets the swamp on fire,
he runs faster, ascends higher. Such lightness,
father, as you would never know on earth.

VIRGINIA OTTLEY CRAIGHILL

BENCH SAW

I hate the sound:
like the inside of
an iron beehive.
I'm too young to
know it doesn't
mean welcome.

I watch you trace
pencil-lines into
cedar shakes for
driving through
the screaming
blade: hoping.

I walk further into
myself: writing
words on reams
of wood pulp with
Orion's Belt tied
around my neck.

I miss you at dawn,
even the rank of
kerosene. Waking
in afternoon to a
thundering clap
of a falling tree.

I look out to the
backyard: bare
with stalagmites

of tree stumps
you say I owe too
much wonder.

I hear you feed
the bench saw;
leaving only the
angry din to say
what we won't
to one another.

MATT VEKAKIS

QUEERS ON THE OREGON TRAIL

to Oregon I'm relentless:
on holidays I pull at your
shawl and beg you to play

settler as the men down-
stairs pray for our souls
long before we understand
what it means to be *queers*.

even the room is magic:
austere, New England white,
snow-lined sill mapping

the cylinder glass window
that moans with the sneezing
attic door we pretend is
haunted by the first pioneers.

even the quiet

before the old, angry Compaq
drops us on the high plains,
where we'll purchase two

oxen to drive West toward
the Columbia: pray we
live long enough to see
                    the other side.

MATT VEKAKIS

JOSHUA 7:22 IN THE RUINS

The whole city was an ambush
the summer before we met
& I was disaster provisions.
I lit fires up and down
Meridian, breaking the law
every time the moon
disappointed me, tried
tunneling home dirt by dew
& then you were salve
and I, a walking wound.
I met you and you stopped
my war with the world you
transformed Indiana
darkness into solitude
o, behold, the smoke of the city
has gone up into the sky
and there is no power
in those ruins anymore.

JESSICA JEWELL

LEAH HAMPTON

L eah Hampton's first book, *F*ckface and Other Stories*, was released in July 2020. The twelve powerful, funny, tragic, and surprising stories are set in towns across the Appalachian South—from Western North Carolina to Eastern Kentucky to West Virginia to Tennessee and beyond—and are populated with complex and complicating modern Southern characters who shoulder through precarious and devastating circumstances, often in darkly humorous and subtly rebellious ways. Through these characters Hampton—originally from Eastern Kentucky—interrogates the Appalachian South, what it means to be from here, what it means to love this place. The sense of natural beauty in these modern mountain stories is lush and reverent, and the dual threats of climate change and industry feature prominently.

On a sunny day in November, Hampton and emerging fiction writer Annie Frazier met via Zoom for a pandemic-friendly conversation about Hampton's work. This interview has been lightly edited for length and clarity.

■ ■ ■

ANNIE FRAZIER: You live here in Western North Carolina, and I gather your family comes partly from Eastern Kentucky. Can you talk to me about what draws you to write about this region and its people, and what importance place holds for you in general as a writer?

LEAH HAMPTON: What draws me to write about this region is, yeah, I have a lot of family connection to it, and also I don't know how you can live here and not create something. I often wonder about people who live here—is there anyone who doesn't then take up pottery or start painting or...? It's the kind of place where you want to create. I just feel really compelled to write about it because I live in a naturally beautiful area. But also because the history is so important to me—I'm a history buff—and because of the complexity of it. It's a misunderstood place, and often a marginalized place, and I find that really interesting. So it's just this perfect storm of beauty and complexity and marginalization that makes it a really good subject, especially for fiction, but for any art.

Leah Hampton   *photo: Carrie Hachadurian*

I think I'm of the Ron Rash school when it comes to place. I think people are defined by their topography. I think it affects us unconsciously—consciously, too. A lot of the characters in the book are being acted upon by the land, whether they realize it or not, and I think that's very common for a lot of people. You don't realize how much you're affected by the geography of the space that you live in until you really start to examine it. That's really interesting to me. I think if I lived anywhere, I would be writing about the place where I lived.

AF: Your stories cover so much ground when it comes to the damage being inflicted on these mountains by climate change, pollution, and industry. Talk to me about what environmentalism means to you and how you've twined it into these stories.

LH: My first job out of high school was working for Greenpeace, and in my younger days I was quite an eco-warrior—I mean, I wasn't, like, capturing whaling ships or anything. But I was a fundraiser and I worked for the Blue Ridge Parkway and for the National Parks and Conservation Association, things like that. And that was where I learned about a lot about this area specifically. But it's also where I learned about editing, because I had to do a lot of grant writing and stuff like that, so it was this really important apprenticeship in how the world works, and it wound up being important to me professionally and personally.

I've always cared about those things and I've always been interested in nature; I love to hike. And I did my undergrad in history, and some graduate work—I really love to study history. Also I'm a very political person. I ran for local office this year. And so, my whole adult life has been paying attention to environmental issues. Having worked in nonprofit, and then having lived in this place, I see the kind of ground-level—if you'll pardon the pun—personal-level impact that those things can have, the communities that are affected when a chemical company doesn't follow the rules or what-have-you. I've seen those people, I've met those people, and I just kept storing that stuff away.

"Parkway," the story in the book about the park ranger, is based on conversations I had going back to my early twenties with park rangers in the Great Smoky Mountains National Park and on the Blue Ridge Parkway who had all kinds of terrible experiences for which there was no assistance at the time. We don't think of people who work in natural spaces as having to deal with trauma when the reality is that a lot of those people see it more than even some small-town hospitals. So, I have always been interested in it. Part of how I have matured as an adult is being really aware of the environment acting on the individual, so that was what I was compelled to write about.

AF: I was especially drawn to the many women characters who populate this collection. They feel deeply recognizable to me—unique, strange, wholly Southern women finding ways to operate just outside of or around or adjacent to an old system that wants desperately for them to look, sound, and behave the same as maybe their mothers and grandmothers did before them. They're often quiet women who rebel, are shunned, and press on with their strangeness in subtle ways. Talk to me about these modern Southern Appalachian women you've created.

LH: I mean, I think you just described us.

AF: Huh, maybe that's why I like them so much!

LH: I was the weird kid in school—I don't know about you—and everybody told me to be sweet, so I was sweet, and then I wrote a book about it. I've been saying this and saying this, and I've got an article coming out in *Guernica* about this. I love men, and I love mountain men, but I'm so tired of their stories. I'm just tired. The women of Appalachian myth and art are very often desexualized. They're living their lives inside of some man's life, or because of some man, and I'm so tired of it.

I see this as being a very feminine place. And I see rural spaces as matrilineal and as complicated and non-binary. And if you study politics, if you study history, the ways in which our mistakes act upon women usually tell you a lot, long-term, about how a given culture or community is going to survive or not.

So, these little tiny personal moments and these, like you said, "small rebellions" that these women have, I think you can see that in what any woman is writing right now in the twenty-first century. We're all tired of it, and we all know that we're kind of a keystone to how things are really going to work or not for us. So I don't think I'm alone in writing about that. And I felt that it was important. I felt that I wanted to write about and to women. But I was very careful—and my editor was great about this—I said, "There will be no pretty font on the cover. It's not a girly book. I don't want to do that." And with how the cover looks and the title, they obviously understood. I was very lucky. It isn't necessarily just a woman's book, but there is a lot about gender.

AF: That does feel like what a lot of women are writing about right now, and it feels so good to read.

LH: To have someone who's not living her life inside of some man, or if she is, she knows there's something wrong with that. To have women who are complicated. When I do high school visits, I've had students say to me, "Well, but I didn't like her because she's cheating on her husband." And I'm like, "Yeah, women do that. We contain multitudes!" You can still enjoy the story, and you can still think she's right and also recognize that you can have a complicated woman. She doesn't have to fit.

I also get very frustrated by the ways in which we write—or, really, don't write—about women over forty. And how suddenly your body becomes less interesting and there are certain tracks that those characters have to fall into. I was definitely interested in busting that open, because I do think of the physical space of Appalachia as being very feminine and being older—it's one of the oldest places in the world. So, if you're going to talk about older women and an older landscape, there's crossover there, in terms of how we can reimagine it.

AF: Sticking with character, as someone who grew up outside of Appalachia but whose family is from here, so many of these characters are familiar to me in a very specific way. They have a sense of reserve to them, a quietness, a distance between themselves and others, and even a distance sometimes between themselves and their own thoughts and emotions. I feel like it's rare for a writer to capture that very Appalachian reserve so successfully, but you've done it. I'm curious about your process of writing characters who maintain that reserved buffer, both around and within themselves.

LH: I know exactly what you're talking about. You have to remember that my dad's family are from Eastern Kentucky—Harlan County—but my mother's family is British, and that's a whole other kind of reserve. So I have, like, double stiff upper lip. Double emotional distance from my own feelings. Or, squared, I guess it would be. So I'm very aware of that, and I see it in a lot of people.

I really like close third person narration, and one of the conscious decisions I had to make when I was working on this book—because it is political, and it was hard not to be preachy about certain issues—was, not everybody has an internal monologue that is...how can I put this? We don't all have this obsessive kind of educated internal thing where you're aware of your own neuroses and that becomes almost a character in the story. The kind of writing I know Mary Lee Settle would just spit stones at.

But there are people who are just as intelligent but who have been trained emotionally and who, out of necessity, have to distance themselves from their own emotional development or epiphany. I find that fascinating because it's often the result of some kind of socioeconomic or other disparity, or some kind of push on that person, and that push creates tension. So you can be inside of one person and only have their perspective, and yet you can create tension because they're smart enough to know what's happening to them, but they also may not be able to reconcile it. That, to me, is a more interesting voice. It was very much on my mind. Not with every story, but with several stories. I wanted to show that internal process of knowing but not knowing, and the tension that creates inside a person.

AF: In quite a few of these stories, there's a level of familiarity with the details of less-than-common jobs that fascinates me. Could you talk about your research process for stories like these?

LH: Some of them are jobs I've had. Or jobs that people I'm very close to have had. I know people who've worked on industrial farms or worked in meat packing. I was a checkout girl in a supermarket many years ago. I've worked a lot of retail.

I also interview people. I don't always tell them that I'm interviewing them for a book, though, because they tell you more if you don't tell them it's for a book, if you just ask them, "What's that for?" when you point to a tool in their toolbox.

But, having grown up in a working-class family—my father was a mechanic—and having always been around people who had job jobs, I'm very aware of work as being a third of your life, minimum. I see that as being very central to who a person is. What do they do? What do they do with their hands? As my mother would say, how do they earn their crust?

The things I had to research were things like specific types of scientists and scientific research. I had to go to some labs, I had to go to some bio research facilities. Firefighting, I had to look into. I had to learn a lot about beekeeping. So there were things that I had to formally research. And then there were people that I talked to.

But then I think the other component of it was just that I'm a person who—if I go to a wedding and there's a chocolate fountain, I'm the person who stands there and thinks about the girl who's going to have to clean that up when the wedding's over. I'm that person, because I've been that person. I tweeted one time, "It's not that I don't love manly-man movies with car chases, it's that I really love fruit stands."

AF: I remember that tweet!

LH: They always knock over a fruit stand! And I'm standing there going, Frank has spent his whole morning organizing those melons and along comes Al Pacino in a Corvette, and now Frank's got to file an insurance claim. His whole weekend is ruined. I can't focus on the movie. I think about working people a lot, so it's just in my DNA to notice that stuff.

AF: Speaking of research and of movies, I wonder how many of the most deeply place-based stories in this collection required the writerly equivalent of location scouting for a movie. Do you visit the places you write about before or during the writing process to gather the natural details that give these stories such richness, or does a lot of that come from memory of places that are familiar to you?

LH: No one's done this yet, because I think I've managed to preempt it, but there's going to be things where you're going to be like, "Well I live in Kingsport, Tennessee, and I know the hospital isn't on that corner." There are times when I have had to take liberties just so something would fit with what I was trying to do. But I'm really big on scaffolding, and most of the physical places that I'm describing are based on someplace I've hiked, someplace I've driven through. For "Mingo," I had to drive. I was like, "I want to write a story where she goes from Charleston to Harlan." I wanted to be in it. I have to be thinking about a physical space.

For the stories where I don't do that, it's just because it's something that's, as you said, so familiar. I know what the back office of a supermarket looks like because I've worked in them. Things like that I can kind of conjure up. But it either has to be something I'm already really familiar with or some wood that I've already physically been in.

But then, you know, I've never fought a forest fire. I had somebody tell me that they read that story before they knew who I was and they thought I was a firefighter, which was a really high compliment. But I've never been in the woods when there's a forest fire. That was based on talking to people who had. So, I do create things, it is fiction, but I think if you know the area well enough, even if you haven't been to the physical space you're describing, you can create the analog of that thing in your mind.

The other thing I do sometimes is look at people's clothes. Like, if I can't go to a fire, but I can look at your turnout gear, then I can see where the dirt is and where the rubber's melted on your boots and that kind of thing.

AF: The story "Twitchell," tackles issues of pollution, immigration, and community. The main character, Iva Jo, feels like our empathetic guide, though she's often cautious and anxious about her own empathy. Iva's friend Margie, on the other hand, represents a kind of insular, othering, closed-off thinking that both perpetuates harm to locals and denies acceptance to newcomers seeking a life in this region. That dichotomy and division feels familiar and important to highlight. Can you talk about the inspiration for this story and what your aim was for it?

LH: There were several inspirations for that story. I have a lot of friends who live in communities in this region who are my age and a little older who are experiencing health issues. I've met and known people who have had mystery cancers, and we all know what those mysteries are. We know where that stuff came from if you live in certain spaces. So I found that fascinating.

Margie was this manifestation of a big group of women who live here, and their thinking, and their clothing. I thought a lot about her hair—spiky hair—and I felt like I had met her even though I made her up. I felt like I knew her, and if I bumped into her at the supermarket, I would know her name was Margie.

There are so many women that do that, and it's a protective instinct, and it's rooted in that kind of white supremacist training that a lot of Southern women have. I wanted to push against it. This isn't a perfect place and we do have problems with our politics, but also with the way that we treat people, especially migrant populations here, especially people of color. I knew that I couldn't write a book where I appropriated the voice of a person of color, I didn't want to do that, but I thought it was important to interrogate some of the whiteness of Appalachian women. I wish I had done more of it, but I think Margie does a pretty good job, and I think it's the longest story in the collection. I wanted to represent that aspect of Appalachian femininity.

I sometimes wish that I had made her even more complicated, or made her sympathetic in some way, so that you could see why we befriend those women and why we tolerate them. But it's challenging, because that story is trying to do a lot. It took me a long time to write. It took me a long time to find somebody to publish it because it's got maxi pads in it and stuff that editors just don't want to touch. It took a long time. I kept telling my agent, "Just quit sending it to, like, twenty-seven-year-old editors named Kevin. Send it to a magazine where they've got a grown-ass woman running it, you know? She'll get it." And we finally found a place to publish it.

AF: I know you've probably been asked this a million times, but I'd love to hear what it's been like to publish your first book during a pandemic that has brought the world screeching to a halt.

LH: I think it's hard for writers right now, because you want to promote your own work and there's just so much noise. But you're also aware that you're very small in this big, international, global problem. And it's been an election, too, which would've made it equally challenging. I have a friend whose first book came out on the day of Trump's inauguration, so she's been very sympathetic about the pandemic.

But where I've landed on it is I'm still going to talk about myself and I'm still going to talk about stories and I'm still going to promote my stuff. I don't have the same reserve about it, and the reason for that is because I feel weirdly privileged to have had my book come out right now. I'm very aware, as a history buff, that the way that we process trauma is by talking about it and by telling stories. That's what the Iliad is, that's what folklore is, that's what we need as a species. We need to tell stories. That's how we get through difficult situations. I feel very humbled and very honored to be a person who has been telling you a story during this difficult time. I'm like, "Yeah, it's terrible! Let me tell you a story." That's how I've decided to look at self-promotion.

But it's been difficult. There are so many people I wish I could have met. I wish I could've done more in-person events. Ultimately, I'm fine, I'm safe, I'm healthy, and I got to tell you a story at a time when we're all really scared, and that's an honor.

But I know it's hard for people, and I completely understand other writers who are going crazy with it, because, you know, you put in years of work and then this happened. So I don't fault anybody for however they're reacting to it.

AF: Tell me about the bold decision to call this equally bold collection *F*ckface*.

LH: Well, another tweet that I had was, "If you want to find out who really loves and understands you, call your book *F*ckface* and just sit back and wait." Because when I told people who know and love me, "So, um, I think I'm going to

Leah Hampton

F★CKFACE

and other stories

"Up-to-the-minute and instantly classic."
—ELIZABETH McCRACKEN

call the book *F*ckface*," they were like, "Of course you are."
Including my editor, who was so gung-ho. She was like, "Let's
do it. Let's just do it."

Now, the story "Fuckface" got written first. That was one of the first stories that I wrote in the collection, and it was like a child that named itself, like I couldn't not call it "Fuckface," even though I knew it meant it probably wasn't going to get published. There's something about it that organically felt like this is what it's called. And as I finished the book, I realized he was a really important person, my favorite person in the book. He's based on someone I know, and I feel really attached to who that character is and what he represents for me personally and for the region and for the characters in the book. This little bright spot of hope.

I knew the book was coming out in an election year, so the nuance and the politicization of language was important. I wanted to slap people in the face a little bit and have them think they knew what this was going to be, and then realize, "Okay, but that's not what this is." That was the effect I was going for. My editor completely got it and she was really down for it, but because of the way that bookselling works, we had to censor the *u*.

But I'm proud of it, you know? I'm proud of it. I told a local newspaper, "If I'm going to be forty-six when my first book comes out, you're going to remember the name. If I had to wait this long, I'm going to make sure you notice when I finally do it."

AF: I love that every story has a one-word title, like the book itself.

LH: Thanks. That's a Robert Gipe conversation. I knew that I wanted [a] one-word [title], and before the book was finished, Robert Gipe and I had a conversation. You know, he does one-word titles. This was a couple years ago, and we were talking about our work. He said, "If you can't whittle down what you're doing to one word, then whatever it is you're doing, you're not really doing it." And that really stuck with me. I had already kind of committed to one-word titles for this book, and then I was like, "If Gipe says it, it's true, so that's what I've got to do."

AF: Humor is such a crucial element in these stories—dark humor, subtle humor, laugh-out-loud humor. Talk to me about the importance of allowing these stories, even some of the saddest ones, to maintain an edge of funny.

LH: Going back to what we were saying earlier about mountain people, you've got to have a sense of humor if you're going to live this life. So it was indicative of the people I'm writing about, that kind of dark comedy, which I see all the time here. It was representative, but I also think it works as a device when you're writing. Because I am writing about, like, gender theory and environmental destruction and just these hopeless situations where people have cancer. So, as a way to keep the reader engaged, I think it's a good tool for the writer to be like, "It's depressing and terrible and there's butt sex!" to kind of keep you with it. In the world-building, it works on a representative and character level and I think it works in terms of thinking about audience.

And I have a really dark sense of humor, so it's true to my voice also. I think people are often surprised if they meet me or see an event that I do before they read my work, I think people expect the book to be even funnier than it is. And then I like smack you in the face with this thirty-page story about breast cancer. But I write to get all that stuff out of my system, so I think my work is very dark, and that enables me to be, as a person, much lighter. The comedy's going to work its way in because humor is a coping mechanism, and it is for a lot of people, so that felt important to write about.

AF: Okay, last question. I want to talk about Dollywood. In your story, "Sparkle," [originally published in *Appalachian Review*] the narrator is unhappy in her marriage and is enamored with her husband's work partner. She takes him to Dollywood and, in a series of subtly devastating moments I won't give away, discovers he's less enchanted by the place than she is, which is a personal blow to her. So can you talk about setting a story at Dollywood and about centering that glittering, technicolor place so it became an extension of the narrator's emotional self?

LH: As a person of the region, I am of course genetically predisposed to be fascinated by Dolly Parton, right? We all love Dolly and she is really important to all of us. But I'm also fascinated by the fascination with her. What is it about her, and what is it about this hyper-real, plastic version of the thing we already live in? Because that's what Dollywood is. It's like this little snow globe inside of a snowstorm. Why are we so obsessed with that?

I think it's the way in which she herself, in her costume and in her attitude and then in her waterpark and her roller coasters, is just turning the Appalachianness volume up to fifty. And I'm drawn to it because it's so unabashed and it's so self-loving, two things that we—generally speaking, in Appalachia—do not do. We are abashed, as a group. So it's cathartic. She's this walking catharsis.

I have had the experience of being in Dollywood on days when she was in the park, and it's this buzz. It's amazing. So I thought that was a great place to put a person who was emotionally conflicted about, well, pretty much everything in her mountain life. She's not sure about her marriage, she's not sure about her heart, she's not sure about who she is herself, she's not dealing with the grief of her family—all these things she's avoiding that are so rooted in this place. So let me put her in the most heightened version of this place I can put her in, and see what happens.

The inspiration for that story really was to retell the James Joyce story, "Araby," because I have always thought that James Joyce would've loved Dollywood. If we could get a time machine and go get James Joyce, he'd be like, "Take me to Dollywood."

AF: As I read it, I realized that a person's reaction to Dollywood—and especially to Dolly's childhood house in the middle of all that shine and plastic—can tell you a lot about them, and I appreciate that you took a place that's easy for people to make fun of and you made it more important than that.

LH: If you go to a place like Dollywood and you can't see us there, then you're never going to see us. And I find that so interesting. The way that we are just so obsessed with her. Across political lines, all over the region, everybody has this thing about that place. I'm academically very interested in that. And also personally. I kind of want to write another story about Dollywood.

There are two things that didn't make it into that story— it's already kind of a long story. I really wanted to write about the little church, too, and I really wanted to write about the bird sanctuary, which is near that church. If I were to go back and write it, I think about the idea of her sitting there with this guy, you know, and an owl just swooping over her head in the bird sanctuary, and what that would mean. But it felt like too much to try to do all that. There's so much about that place— somebody needs to write a whole book about it. ■

NOSTALGIA

The sun feels smaller now.
Ivy browns on the buildings while
wind whistles through the cracks
in my window and curls up beside me in bed.

I dream of the days I got drunk
at your aunt's 4th of July picnic
and cried on the drive home
because you wouldn't hold my hand;

when the afternoons were long and unbearable
and didn't trip over one another in haste;
when the distance between us could be measured by a string
and two tin cans. The world was no bigger
than the gaps between our fingers

and even the traffic outside my window
rushed past with a homesick familiarity.

DJ HILLS

BLUE HERON

Is it the squeaky orange plastic of the inner tubes
or the splash of Straw-ber-ita cans
slipping from drunk grips that startles you into flight?

A wild gesture of limbs points you out
nearly invisible against the cloudless horizon,
proof that the sky and earth were lovers once:

blue as summer, feathers
soft and stark as peat moss.
Take me with you! someone calls

as if you would;
as if we have anything
to offer in return.

DJ HILLS

ON A DARK ROAD

Slow down, I said,
I, barely a teen, holding that man's child
a man I thought I loved,
love being the most misguided word,
love neither what he did nor gave.
He drove down a dark, twisting road
surrounded by pines
Slow down.
You're going to hit a deer.
His look of irritation
slung towards me like a slap,
the sweat of his son's flesh against mine
the slam of the brakes,
the busted headlight, broken mirror,
a head against the windowpane.

ROSEMARY ROYSTON

CLINCH RIVER
ASHES

LAURA DEMERS

Through the screen door, she saw Ruby sitting with her legs on the sofa.

"Knock, Knock," called Paulette.

Ruby picked up the remote and muted the TV. "Come on in!"

A fly followed Paulette inside. The day was so bright that it took a moment for her eyes to adjust to the indoors. The dryer was going, and as she passed through the kitchen to the sitting room she saw a small pot of pinto beans on the stovetop.

"You hungry, honey?"

Ruby had a heating pad over her right calf. Her varicose veins always made Paulette feel weak. They bulged, greenish and blue along her lower legs, under her papery skin.

"My damn leg is giving me trouble!" she said with mock fury.

"Again? What have you got on TV?"

A drag queen was on a panel show. He was speaking to a woman with a helmet of blonde hair and tired eyes.

"Do you know that's a *man*?" said Ruby, waving at the screen. She unmuted it and they listened to them talk about fashion trends.

"Well, Aunt Ruby, I think I'll get started."

"Sure, honey. You know where everything is. I've got a new roll of paper towels under the sink. And don't forget to vacuum under the upstairs bed this time!"

Her aunt had hired her to do some cleaning around the house. She was grateful for the money, but Ruby was a perfectionist. Each time Paulette arrived, there would be a fresh admonishment. She'd left dust on the dresser or she'd forgotten to put in the fabric softener.

"I wish I still had the energy to do it myself," she would always say.

Ruby was actually her great-aunt, her grandmother Wanda's sister. She was in her early eighties and had lived a life totally foreign to them. She never went to church and she had been married five times, only once to someone from West Virginia. The rest of her husbands had been from places like Texas and Florida and New Jersey. On the dresser in her bedroom was a photo of herself with the New Jersey husband, who had been a pilot for Eastern Airlines. She wore a string of pearls in the photo and her hair was long and crimped and parted on the side like an old movie star. Paulette would stare at the photo, trying to imagine Aunt Ruby as this woman and not the woman on the sofa with the shriveled arthritic hands and seamed face.

Ruby was separate to them. They would pray for her, but Paulette's mother would also gossip about her and sometimes even hide from her when she saw her car come up to the trailer.

Today, Paulette stripped her bed, which had a heating pad, too, plugged into the wall. Ruby seemed to sleep so still as to hardly muss the sheets. Her sheets were a crisp blue under a white knit bedcover. Around the bedroom were other photos of her life beyond West Virginia. Her younger daughter when she was a teenager, her son in his military outfit, the older hippy daughter who had died in Haight-Ashbury in the sixties.

Paulette examined the picture of the older daughter now as she shook a pillow from its case. The daughter looked a little like Ruby in the picture with her New Jersey husband, the same eyes and high cheekbones. She had long blonde hair and wore a Shetland sweater and a pair of round wire-rimmed glasses. It was a black and white photo, but her eyes behind the eyeglass lenses were so light you knew they were blue.

Paulette had heard she had died of a drug overdose. She wanted to know about her, but it seemed wrong to bring up a dead child. Paulette's grandmother would still cry if you asked about her baby that died in her arms, and that was easily half a century ago.

As Paulette carried the bed sheets through to the washing machine, Ruby said, "What grade will you be this fall?"

"Tenth," said Paulette.

"Smart girl. Wanda and I never had any schooling. Did she tell you that?"

"Yes."

The drag queen was no longer on TV. Now it was a thin dark-haired woman with oversized sunglasses.

"I went to school once when I was your age for about two months, and then my mother said she needed me back at home."

"Did Mamaw go with you?"

Ruby frowned. "You know, I don't remember. I left town soon after." She waved her arm. "I said to myself, what's over that hill? And then I went and found out."

Paulette smiled and went to put the sheets in the machine.

"Don't forget the fabric softener this time!" called Ruby.

"No, ma'am."

When she had finished upstairs, she came down to find Ruby making a grilled cheese sandwich with tomatoes.

"You didn't think I was going to feed you pinto beans, did you? I remembered you liked it with jalapeno cheese. Help yourself to some soda."

Ruby's back was hunched with osteoporosis, and she always leaned with one hand on something: the back of a chair, a counter top, the wood frame of the doorway.

"I think I'm done upstairs. I didn't change the sheets."

"No need," said Ruby. "Wait 'til I have a guest."

She flipped the sandwich in the pan and waved away the fly with the spatula.

When the sandwich was ready, she put it on a plate and gave Paulette a paper napkin. She sat down opposite and watched her eat it, looking exhausted with the effort.

"Robin might be coming for Christmas," she said.

"Really?" said Paulette, her mouth full.

"With her boyfriend. He's a truck driver. Damn near always on the road. They've been together seventeen years now."

The TV was turned down, but Paulette could hear the applause of a studio audience.

"I sure miss my Robin," said Ruby.

"She looks so young in that picture on your dresser."

"She was maybe your age now. Fifteen."

Paulette swallowed and wiped her mouth. "And same with your other daughter in her picture?"

She held her breath, but Ruby did not pale or start to cry.

"Shelley? Oh, I'm guessing she was a year or two older."

Paulette waited, but Ruby just sighed.

"She died young, didn't she?" Paulette prodded.

"She sure as hell did," Ruby snapped. "Got mixed up in drugs. What a waste. Do you know she was top of her class? Straight A student."

"I bet you miss her."

Ruby shut her mouth tight and stared out the kitchen window. After a moment she said, "Oh, it hurts too much to talk about. I kicked her out. Did you know that? She was doing drugs in my home. I told her to get the hell out if she was going to do drugs."

Paulette gasped.

"Yeah, try to live with that." Ruby shook her head and took a sip of milk, her fingers trembling. "We're all just here to break each other's hearts."

■ ■ ■

When Paulette got to Dwayne's, he was nowhere to be found. She could tell he had been there not long ago. A half bottle of beer sat on the sink counter, still a little cold.

She helped herself to it and went back outside. It was summer, still light at seven o'clock. She sat on the cinder blocks leading up to his trailer and waited until the sky was a burnt orange and fireflies began to glow. A pair of Dwayne's boots sat in the dirt, their shoelaces caked with mud. Inside one of the boots was a wrapper for a PayDay.

The mangy dog from two trailers down slinked in the twilight towards her.

"Hello, Slinky."

She had named the dog herself. When he saw her, he would come as close as fifteen feet and then drop to his belly and slink to her the rest of the way, his ears back along his skull. He had soft brown eyes and white paws, and part of his tail was missing.

At last Dwayne's car pulled up. He had Lester in the passenger seat.

"Where you all been?" she called.

Slinky ran off as they approached.

When Dwayne got out, he said, "Over at my cousins."

"I told you I'd be back at seven."

"Is that my beer?"

Dwayne pushed past her into the trailer. She followed him in, ignoring Lester. Dwayne went to the fridge and then turned to her with a face of heartbreak.

"That was my last beer."

Dwayne went and flopped down on the sofa, his arm arranged on the back of it, an invitation for her to sit next to him. She smiled and hurried over.

"We'll send Lester to get us some more," she said.

Dwayne went and flopped down on the sofa, his arm arranged along the back of it, an invitation for her to sit next to him. She smiled and hurried over. He smelled of sweat and Right Guard. She put her face into the crook of his arm and took a deep breath.

"That can't smell good," he said. "You are crazy, girl."

He kissed her and she could taste the deodorant and his sweat in both their mouths.

Lester appeared in the doorway.

"Let's not put on a show for Lester," said Dwayne.

Lester stood with his arms hanging loose, his eyes glassy.

"I don't care what y'all do," he said, and turned and wandered back outside.

"Lester's not good for nothing right now."

Paulette sighed. "I'll go." She stood up and held out her hand.

"I thought you just did cleaning for that crazy aunt of yours."

"She's going to pay me Friday."

Lester grumbled and reached into his pocket. He pulled out a ten and three singles.

"Get us a six pack and get me a PayDay," he said.

She looked at him closely. "Did you start?"

"Nah."

She let herself out. Lester was laying on the back seat of the car, with his feet planted on the ground.

"I'm going to the corner store," she told him.

He lifted his hand.

"You want anything?"

When he didn't answer she carried on up the road. It was only a five-minute walk. The last of the sun was being swallowed up by the hills in the distance. The road was mostly quiet until an eighteen-wheeler started towards her. She hugged the shoulder of the road, feeling its vibration as it passed, a shuddering effect that made her teeth chatter.

When she reached the store, a man was pumping gas into his Ford. He had a bag of Kentucky Fried Chicken on the roof of his car, which he ate with his right hand while he held the pump with his left.

Inside, the store was empty. She wandered the aisle under the humming florescent lights. She picked up a PayDay for Dwayne and a Three Musketeers for herself. Everything was coated in a sticky film of dust and the lights fritzed and blinked.

She wished she had walked a little farther to the Circle K, which was only ten minutes in the opposite direction. Sometimes the candy bars here were old and moldy when you opened them.

She unwrapped the Three Musketeers. Sure enough the chocolate had turned a crusty white.

"If you open that you better buy it," said the boy behind the counter. He was a few years older than Paulette with pustules of acne along his jaw and his neck. He was tall and rangy and had mean eyes behind his glasses.

"It's no good," she said, holding it up. She brought it to the counter. "Look. The chocolate is all old."

"Don't matter. You still got to buy it if you don't want me to call the police."

"Harvey used to let me check first."

"Well, Harvey's gone now, ain't he?"

"So I guess you're not going to let me buy any beer either?"

"Not unless you suddenly turned twenty-one." He scratched his neck and fiddled with the cash register.

"Fine." She slammed down the candy bars and reached over for a couple of beef jerky rolls from the box. "I should have gone to Circle K."

It was an empty threat. They wouldn't sell her beer there either.

As he was ringing her up, he said, "Got robbed last night around midnight."

"No!" she breathed.

"Didn't you hear no cop cars?"

"Come to think of it, I did."

She had been fast asleep at midnight and heard nothing, but she hated that she had missed it.

"Who was it? Did they have a gun?"

"*Yeah*, they had a gun. They got everything in the register. It was a professional job."

"My mother told me the liquor store was robbed last month. Were you scared?"

He took a paper bag out and shoved her candy bars and the beef jerky into it. "I wasn't working." He looked a little ashamed.

"You weren't?"

"No. Sheryl was here."

"The lady with the short hair? Is she all right?"

"She's shook up."

Outside, the fat man was still leaning against his car and finishing his dinner. He lifted a drum leg in greeting as she passed.

She took her time getting back to the trailer, hoping Dwayne wouldn't send her right back out to Circle K to take her chances there.

■ ■ ■

Before she went over to her aunt's the next day, Paulette went to see Dwayne's cousin at the pharmacy next to Food Lion. Kara was almost twenty and had dyed blonde hair and had dropped out of school early to have a baby, but the baby had died. Her eyes were a dull pale brown, the color of dirty mop water, an ugly feature in an otherwise pretty, doll-like face. Paulette would stare at her and try to take in every detail. The multiple earring studs up and down her ears, her black choker necklace, her clumpy mascara, her way of holding her shoulders as if she were protecting herself.

Kara always let her have a free candy bar. She would glance quickly at the pharmacist and then wink at Paulette.

Paulette had seen her around town since she was little, but she hadn't known Kara to speak to until she and Dwayne became a couple. Now when she'd go into the pharmacy, the bell would ring and she'd wander up and down the aisles, past the Whitman's chocolate boxes and the greeting cards over to the boxes of denture cleanser and the contact lens solution to the heating pads and the Ace bandages. When it was clear of customers, she'd go up to the counter.

Today the store was empty so she went straight to the counter where Kara was painting her nails. She was putting a clear varnish over a layer of iridescent pink.

"What do I want for lunch?" said Kara, without looking up.

"A Subway sandwich?"

Kara put the brush in the bottle and shook her fingers. "Nah. I want a strawberry shake. Run on over to Sonic Burger. I can't get my money out without ruining my nails."

Paulette went behind the counter and dug a few dollars out of her purse.

"Bring me change!" she called as Paulette headed back out.

Getting Kara's lunch was one of the great joys of Paulette's summer. Kara would either ask for a six-inch roast beef sandwich with onions and tomatoes from Subway, a spicy chicken burger from Wendy's, or a milkshake from Sonic Burger. Sometimes she wanted a combination of all three, which would require Paulette to walk the half-mile radius encompassing all the different fast food chains that dotted two sides of the road between the turn off for the interstate and the bank.

Today it was almost ninety degrees. She turned to look longingly at the municipal pool on the other side of the parking lot. Through the chain link fence she saw a group of small children and a large girl in a hot pink one-piece bathing suit.

At Sonic Burger an older man watched her from a plastic seat as she ordered. He had a salt and pepper mustache and took large bites of his hamburger, his eyes leaden with lust.

She stood with her back to him, feeling his gaze on her bare legs like the toxic rays from a sun lamp.

When she was headed back out the door with Kara's milkshake, he called, "What flavor you get?"

Paulette stopped. "Strawberry."

He had a trucker hat next to him on the table. It read Canon's Dairy.

"Good choice. I always get chocolate," he said. "You got yourself a fella?"

"Yeah," said Paulette.

He winked and she pushed through the glass doors. When older men flirted with her in public, which they had now for almost two years, she felt a thrill of power, as if she could crush them with her bare hands.

In private, it was different.

Dwayne would never be like that. He was too gentle to ever get rough or hiss dirty things in her ear. The only time he'd made her cry was when he said he might join the Marines. She had sobbed big swollen tears as they watched TV, but nothing had ever come of it, and it didn't frighten her anymore when he brought it up.

Kara was busy with customers when she got back to the pharmacy. Paulette set the milkshake on the counter and began the two-mile walk to Aunt Ruby's.

Today, Ruby had her clean the kitchen and Windex all the windows.

"You're leaving streaks, honey," said Ruby. "If I had any energy I'd show you how to do it right."

Paulette was wiping the glass next to a spider plant in the sitting room. Out the window a hummingbird was suspended in midair, darting at the birdfeeder.

"How much more of summer have you got left?" asked Ruby.

"Three more weeks."

"Have you thought about what you might do when you graduate? Maybe you'll go to the community college."

Paulette kept her back to her. She folded the paper towel in half and slid it in patterns along the left pane of the window.

"If I were you, I'd get all the schooling I could. Did you know I once took your father with me out of here to Florida?"

Paulette turned around. "You did?"

"When he was ten."

"Away from Mamaw?"

"Yep. Just put him in the car with us and then put him into school down there."

"Wasn't everybody mad at you?"

"I didn't *kidnap* him."

"I didn't know he ever lived anywhere but here."

She nodded. "He did. He lasted until almost Christmas and then his mother said she missed him too much." She shook her head in disgust. "He was on his way to getting a real education."

She seemed to expect some reaction from Paulette.

"I guess he was real homesick, too," said Paulette.

"He would have got over it."

Later, while they ate lunch in the kitchen, Ruby said again, "Yep, if I were you, I'd get all the education I could. Your mother says you get good grades."

Paulette nodded.

Ruby leaned forward, her elbows on the table. "I could help with the tuition if you wanted to go."

Paulette stared at her. "You'd give me money?"

"Sure. Do you think you might like to do that? Go to community college?"

"I hadn't thought of it."

"Why not?"

"Because Dwayne's here."

"Dwayne!" She snorted and took a sip of her milk. "You need to get away from here like I did. I could always tell you were smarter than the rest."

Paulette was mystified, but said nothing.

"I gave your father a chance to get out and make something of himself. Maybe he was too young. But you have a good head on your shoulders. That's what your mother says."

"She just thinks that because I'm in the marching band."

"Well, I'm a good judge of character. You get away from that piss ant Dwight and work hard on your grades and I can help you with community college."

"Dwayne," said Paulette.

"What?"

"You called him 'Dwight.'"

Ruby leaned and took a spoonful of her soup. Her dentures dropped and she pushed them back into place with her forefinger.

"Do you know when I was younger than you are now, I wanted to get out of here so bad that when a man came through town and said he would take me with him, I decided to go."

Paulette thought of the man at Sonic Burger, of his mustache with the smear of mayonnaise in it.

"You did?"

"Yep."

"How old were you?"

"Fourteen."

"So what happened?"

"I packed up and went to the train station and he never showed up. Can you imagine that?" Her eyes blazed with outrage.

"Maybe it was for the best. Maybe he would have killed you, or worse."

She waved her hand. "Oh, I could take care of myself. I was meaner than a snake even then." She shook her head wistfully. "Yeah, that was a real heartbreak."

When they were done, Paulette put the dishes in the sink and watched Ruby make her way back to the sofa. Her housedress was unzipped a few inches at the top, so Paulette could see the knobby top of her spine where it curved over and a scattering of thick, dark moles. As she lowered herself carefully back to her perch on the sofa, Paulette's back ached in empathy.

"You'd really do that for me?" she said more to herself than out loud.

Ruby looked over and jabbed her finger at her. "You bet I would. I know a smart kid when I see one."

She turned up the volume on her murder mystery.

"Tell me this," she yelled over the TV. "Why doesn't someone investigate the old broad on this show? Wherever she goes, people drop dead!"

"Ha!" said Paulette. "Ha."

■ ■ ■

"Kara got fired."

Their TV had broken so Dwayne was throwing darts at the dartboard, which he had propped up on a low table against the wall. Every few minutes he'd heave himself up and pull them out of the board and start again.

Paulette stared at him. "What happened?"

"She got caught stealing, that's what."

"Candy bars?"

Ruby had asked her to come in earlier every day that week, so Paulette hadn't been to the drugstore in three days.

He turned to look at her. "*Candy* bars? Money!"

"I didn't know she was stealing money."

"She says she wasn't, but I know she was. She says it was the other girl there who did it."

"I believe her," said Paulette.

"That's because you're dumb." He reached over and chucked her under the chin. "She's coming over."

Paulette gathered the beer bottles from the table and put them in a paper bag and took them outside. The early evening air was soothing after a scorching day. She was sorry Kara had been fired. She wouldn't get to visit her at the pharmacy anymore. Still, she was excited to hear the story of what had happened.

"Where's Lester?" she called through the open door.

"He'll be here sometime. Aren't you going to sit with me?"

It was so hot in the trailer. Dwayne couldn't feel it because he had been snorting his stash. One time, she had spilled bacon grease on him by accident and he had not even flinched.

"I was thinking about going down and applying for that job at the mall in Princeton," he called. "At the movie theatre. I could sneak you in to see movies for free. I bet they'd give me a discount."

She turned to watch him through the doorway, admiring his delicate profile in the lamplight. Just then Kara's car pulled

She stepped out of the car, her legs lean and spidery, and pulled up her halter top.

up, an old brown Buick her stepfather had given her. She stepped out of the car, her legs lean and spidery, and pulled up her halter top.

She smiled at Paulette. "I guess you heard."

"It wasn't my fault, was it? Because of the candy bars?"

Kara took a pack of cigarettes out of her shoulder bag. She lit one and then sauntered towards her.

"Yep, that was it. All them candy bars." She took a long drag of the cigarette and gazed down at Paulette, letting the smoke curl out of her mouth.

Dwayne got up and came to the door.

"Where's Lester?" she asked.

"I don't know. He should be here by now."

She smoked dreamily for a few moments. They both waited.

"Well, let's go get him, then," she said finally. "I don't have all night."

■ ■ ■

Paulette had a sinking feeling all the way there. She'd only been to the holler where Dwayne's cousins lived once before, the day school finished, after she had been seeing him for two months.

She sat in the backseat now, behind Dwayne and Kara, and rested her head against the cool glass of the window. She concentrated on the black roots of Kara's head and thought that at least there would be another girl with her this time. The road curved back and forth through the thick soft trees, and even as slowly as Kara was driving, Paulette began to feel carsick.

They finally pulled off a dirt road near the top of the holler and parked behind two trucks. One was a broken down Chevrolet and another was a bright white 4x4 Explorer.

When Kara got out of the car, Paulette leaned forward and plucked at Dwayne's sleeve.

"I don't feel so good," she said.

"What do you mean?" His eyes were so dilated they looked black.

"Something's wrong with my stomach."

"They'll give you something inside for it."

"Let's go back, Dwayne."

"What's the matter? Come on."

He brushed her hair back from her face. Through the windshield she saw Kara's silhouette in the fading light. She had her hand on her hip, but there was a deadly patience about her. There was nothing Paulette could do but follow them.

They walked over a thin board across a brook to the property. It was a large ramshackle construction, part house, part shed. On the side porch sat two broken washing machines, an empty dog kennel, a shovel, and a bag of fertilizer.

When they stepped inside, it was pitch black, as if the house swallowed light. Kara flipped on a switch and the first thing Paulette saw was the Jesus icon on the wall and next to it a framed certificate that read *The United States of America* with a ribbon and a star.

In the next room sat two men and Lester, his head lolling to its side, his eyes closed.

"What y'all doin?" said the man closer to the door. He held up his hand and Kara smacked it listlessly as she passed. He was Kara's brother Clay. The other brother, Richard, was in his thirties. He sat on a plaid sofa with the stuffing coming out of it, in front of a low wooden table. At first, he did not seem to register them.

The two brothers had the same refined features in their long faces as Dwayne and Kara. The older brother was missing an arm from Iraq. He wore a sleeveless black sweatshirt so that Paulette could see the puckered scar where his arm had been.

"Lester here is done," said Richard, staring straight ahead.

"We think he's been Oxycuted," said Clay.

Paulette was so relieved to find only two of them tonight. In June, there had been at least three other men, one who never took his eyes off her, even though Dwayne had been stroking her hair the whole time.

Kara reached into her purse now and pulled out a wad of cash and a bottle of pills. Paulette's mouth gaped open, but she quickly clamped it shut.

Clay took the bottle of pills and examined the label and took one out. He crushed it with the end of a kitchen knife. Then he took a little water from a syringe on the table and mixed it in the palm of his hand. He filled the syringe again with the liquefied pill and found a vein on his arm. He pressed it until it filled with blood.

His eyes flickered shut and then Paulette watched Dwayne do the same thing for himself, from the same bottle of pills. Kara's expression as she watched them was suddenly soft, as if with maternal pride at what she had done for them.

"Where'd you get that shirt?" asked Kara, when she saw Paulette looking at her.

"Magic Mart," said Paulette.

Kara offered her a pill, but she shook her head.

Dwayne said, "This ol' aunt of hers told her to just say no."

They all burst into cheerful laughter.

"Her little girl died shooting heroin," said Dwayne.

"You don't say," said Richard, finally registering Paulette.

Dwayne stretched out his legs. "She's that crazy old lady lives on Pisgah Road. She sure is crazy. She ran away to Miami when she was fifteen."

"Charlotte," said Paulette.

"What?"

"She went to Charlotte first."

"She got married *six* times."

"Five," said Paulette.

"And her daughter died out in San Francisco. She was one of them hippie freaks."

They were all watching Paulette now, detached, curious.

"Her house sure is nice," said Kara. "I've seen it from the outside."

Something was pecking at the side of the house. Paulette heard a chain rattle and then the bark of a dog.

Around the room, everything was gathered in piles. Toaster ovens in a pile. Framed pictures in a pile. Boots in a pile. Even two old TV sets had their own pile, a china figurine of an angel with wings perched on top of them.

Paulette shrugged. "It's nothing special."

Richard leaned forward on his one arm, resting his elbow on his knee. Under his sleeveless sweatshirt, a small roll of fat appeared around his waist and pressed against his belt. It seemed the only soft spot on him.

"Where'd you say it was?"

"Pisgah Road," said Kara, absently. She got up and peered at herself in a small mirror that spelled out the word Schlitz over it.

"Paulette cleans for her," said Dwayne. "You should hear the stories she tells Paulette. Even Paulette's mom hides from her when she comes over to visit."

"That's not true," said Paulette.

"That's what you told me."

The smell of his Right Guard came off him so thick and sickly sweet she wondered if she might be ill.

"My stomach don't feel so good," she said.

"Ah, shit. You better not be pregnant," hooted Clay.

Richard was still watching her, his expression thoughtful. Kara turned from the mirror and looked first at Richard and then at Paulette. Paulette was reminded of a time she had gone to the woods with her uncle and they'd come upon three deer with large dark shining eyes. She'd been too young then to know the deer would run, and for a long terrible moment she had waited for them to pounce.

"Do you have a key to her house?" asked Kara.

Paulette pretended not to hear her. "I'm not pregnant," she said. "I'm just a little sick feeling, that's all."

"We know you're not pregnant, honey," said Richard softly. "Besides, even if you was, Dwayne here would take care of you, wouldn't you, Dwayne?"

"Hell, yeah," he said. "I'm gonna join the Marines."

Clay took a bottle cap and tossed it across the room at Lester, who came out of his slumber like a sleepy baby, drool shining on his chin. He looked around and blinked and smiled as if they'd gathered there to surprise him.

"You know what old ladies got a lot of?" said Richard. "Money and medicine. Paulette, does your aunt have either of those things laying around?"

Paulette stood up quickly. She pulled at Dwayne's arm. "I need to talk to you for a second."

"What are y'all up to?" murmured Lester.

She pulled Dwayne outside, tripping over the shovel and banging her knee on the leg of an upended table.

"Where's the fire?" he asked.

"Dwayne, you tell them to leave Aunt Ruby alone."

"You know what old ladies got a lot of?" said Richard. "Money and medicine."

He shushed her and then moved his hips into hers, putting his arms tightly around her shoulders. She felt herself relax into him. She could feel his slow beating heart through his T-shirt.

"Let's go home," she said. "I don't mind walking."

"Now don't get all upset," he said soothingly into her hair. "You don't really think you're pregnant, honey?"

"I just got my period."

"Well, then that's fine."

"I want them to leave Aunt Ruby alone."

Richard came to the door. "What are y'all doing out here?"

Dwayne took a step back from her and dropped his arms.

"Y'all come back inside," said Richard. "I need to ask Paulette some questions."

"Please, Dwayne," muttered Paulette.

"This is my family, girl," he said. "Richard practically raised me. Didn't you, Richard?"

"I'd give you the one arm I have left, Dwayne. You know that. Now you two come on back inside."

■ ■ ■

In the dark, the furniture made looming shapes. When Paulette turned she saw someone coming towards her and almost shrieked before she realized it was herself in the mirrored living room closet. She had taken the key from the potted geranium plant and come through the front. It was further away from Ruby's bedroom than the side door.

When she was digging for the key outside, she had heard the truck idling behind her. It had occurred to her to pretend the key wasn't there. But she knew it wouldn't be the end of it, they would come back the next night or the next.

She turned on the small flashlight and swung it over the room, to the framed photos on the bookshelf, to the crude painting of an Appalachian autumn, a deer in the foreground. She aimed the flashlight at the mirror and saw her own ghostly face, her denim skirt, her lumpy sweater.

She had dusted and vacuumed this room a handful of times, had stared at the photos, lined up carefully in metal frames. She aimed the flashlight and saw the son on leave from Vietnam in Hawaii, his sweet-faced wife in an A-line skirt; the daughter Robin holding a cat in a snowy driveway; a black and white of the hippie daughter when she was a girl with an Alice headband and glasses.

Paulette moved to the kitchen. The smell of Ruby's cornbread dinner hung in the air. When the front door shut gently, she aimed the flashlight at it.

"Who's there?"

"It's me," whispered Kara.

Paulette hissed at her to go back to the truck.

Kara came into the kitchen. "It'll be faster if we work together."

"You don't even know this house. Let me do it on my own."

Kara was close enough now that she could smell the gum on her breath.

"Two pairs of hands are swifter than one," said Kara. She took the flashlight from Paulette. "Where does she sleep?"

■ ■ ■

After Kara had helped herself to one of Ruby's Cokes and moved off upstairs with the flashlight, Paulette was left in the dark. She stood at the kitchen sink and looked out over the back of the property, a half-acre down to the river. Ruby had told her that when she died, she wanted her ashes sprinkled in that river.

"Although I hear it's full of poison now and is probably the thing that is killing me."

Moths spun and sizzled against the outside porch light. Paulette could see a spiderweb spun across the beams of the corner of the window. The spider trembled in the breeze.

Upstairs she heard the creak of Kara's footsteps. A moment later, Kara came back down and moved past her like a shadow to the bathroom in the hall. Paulette heard cabinets softly opening and closing. When Kara came back in the kitchen, she rattled a bottle of pills.

"What are these?" she whispered.

"It's her blood pressure medicine." Paulette's voice was flat with hate. She could smell that Kara had sprayed herself with Ruby's Yves Saint Laurent cologne.

"Well, I found some liquid codeine and a half a bottle of Xanax. Where does she keep her valuables?"

"I'll get them myself. You go on back to the truck now."

"Ooh, look at you, giving me orders," said Kara in a sing-song voice.

"They're in the bedroom, and it's too hard to explain. You'll wake her up."

"Fair enough." She reached forward to the windowsill where a porcelain swan sat and put it in her purse. "What's with that big old TV? It looks like something from the year Jesus was born."

When Paulette didn't answer, Kara clicked the flashlight on her face, and then off, and then on and then off. Then she leaned forward and gave her a kiss on the cheek.

"I got her money anyway. It was in her Bible," said Kara. "All old ladies are alike. See you in the truck. Don't take too long."

She turned the flashlight on Paulette's face one more time, making her flinch. Then she handed it to her and slid out of the room. A moment later, Paulette heard the front door squeak on its springs.

Paulette went into the sitting room and lingered there with the flashlight off. She could see everything in her mind's eye. The old-style television, the silk flowers in the beveled glass vase, the spider plants, the air conditioning unit, the sofa with its heating pad placed against the pink sofa pillow, the packet of saltines in the glass bowl, a spiral notebook with the list of phone numbers scrawled in emphatic writing: Dr. Mead, Bank, Dan in Florida, Post Office, Robin in Maryland, Wanda, Hospital, Paulette.

Finally, she went down the hall to Ruby's bedroom. The door was open and she felt a breeze from the north-facing window. In the faint light through the window, she could see Ruby asleep on her side.

She got down on her hands and knees and felt for the shoebox in the closet where she knew Ruby kept her son's dog tags, her daughter's graduation ring, the string of pearls from the Eastern Airlines husband, the picture of her parents. She had found the box one day when Ruby asked her to put a mousetrap back there. When she opened the box, two fierce-looking hillbillies had stared back at her from a sepia-toned photo, the father with Ruby's high cheekbones, the mother with her oval face. Paulette had found a school report in there, too, all A's, and a silver baby rattler.

The box wasn't in the closet anymore.

"Remember to get that pearl necklace," Dwayne had said in front of Richard. She hated herself now for telling Dwayne what she'd found that day.

She sat back and listened to Ruby's breathing, then turned and shined the flashlight under the bed. There was the JCPenney shoebox next to a blanket in a clear plastic zip bag. She moved over to the side of the bed and eased the shoebox out. With the flashlight off, she felt inside for the pearls and carefully put them in her pocket.

When she lifted her head, Ruby was staring at her in the dark, her eyes wide and still. Another gust of cool air passed through the room, bringing with it the smell of the pine outside. Its branches scratched against the open window.

Ruby was so motionless that if it weren't for her breathing, Paulette would have thought she was dead. She wanted to ask her questions that she would never be able to ask again, about her dead daughter and Miami and the man who had never shown up at the train station.

They stared at each other for a full twenty seconds, Paulette's stomach like ice. When Ruby finally blinked, Paulette whispered, "Go back to sleep, Aunt Ruby."

Outside the truck was waiting. ■

THE POET STUMBLES UPON A USED HYPODERMIC NEEDLE WHILE FISHING IN SCHUYLKILL COUNTY

after Todd Davis

and quickly, finally notes how the sun has rested

behind the hill, and how shadows of rhododendron

are now covering everything, and how the deep run underneath

the far bank where he caught a brown trout with a brake light

red adipose fin is perfectly watched from the syringe's resting spot,

and how this is a good place to be alone, between the railroad tracks

the river the woods the highway and Adult Shop 61 and at least

they put the cap back on and maybe they love the way this nook

MICHAEL GARRIGAN

feels like being somewhere-completely-else in an unrelenting

wildness as much as he does and he wonders if this is from the guy

he saw crawl from the tent downstream behind the burnt-out hotel

which makes him think about the economy and how there used to be jobs

around here back when these woods were rusty thin, lining factories burning

but the darkness is getting fuller, heavier, and his truck is a ways

upstream and he no longer wants to be alone nor does he want

to meet someone back here so he makes one last roll cast and strips

the black woolly bugger back, not even letting it jig or drift

a bit before he reels in and wades across the stream.

ROWING OUT OF A RIPTIDE

I.
whiskey-blurred Panhandle mutterer
    rowing canoe over eelgrass
toothpicking his Lake City
        lowland youth
like wild blackberry
            strumming trail myths
from memory hammering
                porch floorboards up a key
patching drywall or driving nails
                half-an-inch into the lonely
                ghost of some lost saint
stuck as a fly on a honeytrap windowpane
            you know he's working Thomas
Street doubt-houses poorer than a churchmouse
        shelling peas in an echo bucket
fixing to fix-up more unending babble

II.
While straw-thin litterboys collected ditch
bottles to cash-in for mint-chocolate-chip
    slide nickels on a dimestore countertop,

        my first conscious fleck happened
    afloat a milk jug raft
drifting past the Gulf sandbar

    —the fathermyth swam his flipper palms
against the axis & riptides
    riffed my blue existence into note.

III.
　　Gravity, the power of love—it's all one
tune the godchild's whistling on Time's bridge.

Hovering gatekeepers, the rambling bookworms
　　keep scrolling through your bright disasters.

FORREST RAPIER

CALL A BODY
HOME

MICHAEL ALESSI

It's not the fists of steam that roll from the body when the sow strung up on gambrels spills open. It's not her father stepping inside to cut away what will be chitlins, the skin folding around his shoulders like two wings. The pocket of heat inside the body soothes the bite of the autumn air, reminding him of a long lost night spent slow-dancing with a married woman at a county bar with wood chips on its floors. The smell of the offal is ripe, but sweet to breathe, almost honeyed. He opens his nostrils to it and pictures the woman, the wife of a friend, guiding his hand to cup the full curve of her hip. His knife is sure, not as clumsy as his lumpy hands feel, bearing no sign of the ache that has set into the bones these last few years, and if he nicks himself, he cannot tell.

It's not the buckets of blood her twin nephews lug to the barn together to pour into an earthen trough. The shorter one has it painted down the side of his overalls from losing his grip on the handle. Still, he refuses to quit, afraid, as he has always been, of the secret weaknesses of his body; its smallness and the way it pines for the touch of taller, stronger boys. His brother curses at him to keep his end of the bucket even, so he raises it, raises it too high, and sends blood spilling in the other direction for once.

It's not the black mantle of hair that bobs on the surface of the scalding pan, or the hook her uncle uses to stir the body. He can barely hear the sound of the old-timers bickering about the heat of the fire. Too hot or cold and the hairs will stick. In the water he sees the white shape of his mother when she used to bathe with him in their trailer's tub, a story he has never told his wife, who grew up in a house in a town far from the hollows.

It's not the way the zinc can lids melt and curl from the heat as the giddy neighbor kids scrape away the last black hairs. They weren't here this morning when the sun didn't so much as rise as pause on the edge of the dark woods, until something passing for daylight occurred; when she woke to find the space her mother left behind still empty, six months cold. Recently, she has been testing gestures, such as slapping her brother when he tells her to chew with her mouth closed, hoping to find one that might summon their mother back from her new home. Today, despite her father's protests, she shared her breakfast with the old sow. A last meal. When the coast was clear, her brother, nursing the glow of a stolen cigarette in his gangly fingers, whistled her over to the fence where she and the sow took turns licking globs of oatmeal off a serving spoon. Maybe their father had forgotten the ghostly shape of their mother, years ago, barefoot in her nightdress in the winter cold, spooning the piglet scraps from her plate. Maybe he'd made up his mind that killing something was easier work than caring for it.

It's not the sight of her brother finally leading the pig to the clearing by a rope. Or their father's pistol, granted for the task, hanging in his free hand. It's that the sow lifts her head to the barrel at the sound of his whistle, the one he uses to call her home. ■

ON MOWING OVER A SNAKE

The narrow fellow in the grass
lost his head today.

I, glutton for experience,
stared at the severed tube
     and tubes in tubes
          bleeding.

But his head was gone,
and, without, he seemed base,
     the devil crushed,
        defeated,

like a casualty of revolution.

I mourned a slow day
for the lost head
of a little friend,

as I walked my
measured circles.

M. CHRISTINE BENNER DIXON

MERCY

    I understand it no better now
than that day cars slowed,
to edge around a pigeon
rocking on its back
in the intersection,
one unresponsive wing,
one that pumped in starts,
rowing a half-turn on asphalt
each time a few
endless seconds more

when a rusted station wagon stopped
in traffic, and a young man driving
pushed his door open, not to step out
and move the dying bird,
but to look back and see clearly
as he backed his left rear tire
over its head,
then to check again
moving slowly forward
to see it was dead.

JOSEPH HARDY

BOOK REVIEWS

Wesley Browne. *Hillbilly Hustle.* **Morgantown, W.Va.: West Virginia University Press, 2020. 264 pages. Softcover. $19.99.**

Reviewed by Emily Masters

"Knox Thompson first crossed paths with the man who would ruin him at a poker game above the arcade in downtown McKee, a forsaken place he had made it a point to avoid," Wesley Browne opens his debut novel *Hillbilly Hustle.* He then takes the reader straight into the seedy underbelly of Appalachia's poker-playing, pot-smoking, gun-toting faction when Knox wins the poker game against the wrong kind of folks. Knox, the main character and owner of Porthos Pizza in nearby Richmond, Kentucky, is the unlikely new recruit to deal pot for a villainous drug dealer called Burl and his beefed-up crony, Greek, who cons Knox into exchanging the money he won during the game for a pound of Burl's pot to move. And what better place to deal pot than from a pizza parlor? From the fast-paced poker game of the first chapter, readers will find themselves sucked right into the plot. The energy of the story only ratchets up from there, and it never slows for a moment.

Hillbilly Hustle at turns made me hungry with descriptions of greasy pizza goodness and made my stomach churn with the violence Knox faces at the hands of Greek and Burl when he isn't living up to their business expectations. The violence, however, is never gratuitous. Instead, it makes Knox's increasing indebtedness to Burl all the more urgent. You'll find yourself rooting for Knox, even as you wonder, Will he make it out alive? In true Appalachian self-reliant style, Knox, instead of asking his friends or parents for help, tries to unstick himself, not allowing anyone else help him claw from the pit of deepening debt.

Browne reveals a darker side to Richmond and the surrounding area. Once Knox is sucked into drug dealing, seeing it as a temporary financial fix, it is easy to see how he could find himself trapped. Knox is never meant to succeed; he is meant to be controlled, a card in Burl's hand. Burl plays that hand with skill, nuance, and suspense. You'll never know what he will do next because he holds his cards close to his chest, only ever giving his associates the slivers of his movements and patterns he wants them to see. Knox is all too aware that Burl is beyond the law, buying them off to turn their heads the other way.

While all of Browne's characters are complex and dynamic, Knox is not a particularly likeable main character. He is lazy, self-pitying, and slovenly. Nonetheless, you'll find yourself rooting for him as he fights to keep his greasy yet loveable pizza parlor financially viable. As you read, you'll find yourself imagining what it would be like to be in Knox's shoes: broke, lonely, indebted. He kneads his wounds like pizza dough, growing softer and softer, coming closer to pushing away everyone he knows and loves, everyone who loves him. Burl is a terrifying villain in his shrewd ability to hit where it hurts, both financially and physically.

Knox's friends Rob and Tori, and his girlfriend Donna, are far more likeable. Perhaps what I most wanted from *Hillbilly Hustle* was more of Knox's girlfriend Donna and the other supporting characters. Donna, a tattoo artist, bails on Knox when he grows distant and inconsiderate as he is driven to distraction by his secret side-life. The final straw for her is when Greek and Burl show up at her tattoo parlor as a warning to Knox. Rob and Tori, Knox's co-workers at Porthos Pizza, are more present throughout the narrative, worrying about and supporting Knox even as he falls apart. It is admittedly representative of Knox's self-involvement and fear that even in the novel, other characters serve primarily as a backdrop for Knox's drama.

Hillbilly Hustle is for anyone looking for excitement, adventure, and even a little bit of fear. After so many months cooped up and socially distanced, Browne's novel is a breath of fresh air. There is thrill in the dangers written into the landscape of Browne's Eastern Kentucky. Rewards, Knox learns, do not come free. He gambles more than he bargains for when he wins the poker game against Burl above the arcade in McKee. He loses his friends, his livelihood, himself. As you read, you'll lose yourself in the pages of *Hillbilly Hustle*, and you'll be glad you did.

Thorpe Moeckel. *Down by the Eno, Down by the Haw: A Wonder Almanac.* Macon, Ga.: Mercer University Press, 2019. 136 pages. Softcover. $16.00.

Reviewed by Misty Skaggs

I was born and raised in the backwoods and have spent a lot of time surrounded by natural beauty. I have also felt trapped by these mountains in my lifetime. Truth is, I haven't ever been far from my corner of Eastern Kentucky, so it was a pleasure to join Thorpe Moeckel as he forged his "wonder almanac" and swept me away from an icy morning in a trailer overlooking Grahn Creek and nearer to the living, breathing, rivers of the Piedmont. *Down by the Eno, Down by the Haw* revealed to me a landscape like I've never known before via poetic observation by Moeckel.

His journey seems to call to him, and the landscape demands his attention from the most mundane of places, from the very beginning of the book on a grey February day when he writes, "Tangly places, little creeks, roots, stumps. Groves and glades. Copses. I try to get lost, try to see. See, edgewise, these edgeplaces, and on, into—if lucky—the beyond, the here in it. On the way to the lumber store, I cross the bridge. Slow down, pull off, find a way in." This full-length prose poem made my heart soar, and I found myself thumbing through these pages to revisit certain scenes the same way the heron circles back to its favorite fishing holes.

There's comfort and sustenance to be found in these chapters. One quick trip through these pages certainly won't be enough to take in all the wonders and wade through the dense language. The author has presented this unique ecosystem and its residents, large and small, in the change of each season. In August, "[c]rickets are as goose pimples on its flanks and limbs. They purr, echoes of screeches from brighter greens. Of course they are invisible. They're behind the eyes. They nibble at the ears. The river's wakes grow abdominal, silent with vast communities of spider's trilogies of silk." Through passages like this, Moeckel evokes the sensory experiences of every season.

Down by the Eno, Down by the Haw is packed with intense and organic imagery, but it is not just another prettily penned collection about trees and flowers. Instead the author offers

up a vulnerable and intimate look at
the relationship between humankind
and the natural world. In the process,
Moeckel does not remove himself
from his journey or from its retelling.
He is present and connected to
both the scenery and the reader
throughout, speaking directly to us
about his experiences.

There isn't an omniscient poetic
voice from Moeckel in this work. He is
not speaking from some cloud on high where he can see it all
with perfect clarity. There are no presumptions or assertions
in his observations. The poet is quite simply another part of
the complex ecosystem he is observing. Moeckel is out in the
summer heat battling mosquitoes and smearing himself with
mud that "smells like a pelt, like blood musky and dense." He's
there atop the bluff in the crispness of autumn, watching and
listening as the chaos of a mid-air hunt ensues and "something
crazy happens" when a hawk snatches a frantic songbird from
its flight.

A moment that could be interpreted as a neat example
of natural, predatory order becomes a much more haunting
scene when he writes, "For a moment the voice seems to
belong to the victim, but the vocals last too long." Moeckel
does not turn away from the brutal moments that also hold
wonder, and he treks through the seasons with such intensity
that the reader might feel as though they are sharing the same
hard frost by the end of the book.

If you're looking for an easy bedtime read, this may not be
the book for you. There are difficult waters and thick copses

to navigate. The prose is beautiful but at times seems so heavy you can get mired down. However, if you're looking for a strong current to take you on a lyrical adventure, *Down by the Eno, Down by the Haw* is a worthy read. This book makes me want to pick up a paddle and follow a river somewhere, anywhere it wants to take me, even though I fully expect to get bit by just about every bug known to man. ∎

SELF-PORTRAIT IN A DIRTY MIRROR WITH THE LIGHTS OFF

Shadow shimmers — vibrates in the dark
    the mirror dotted — pocked with stains — splashed
        I see — only faintly — my ragged reflection

flared nostrils — thin rose-colored lips
    gritted teeth — ground finely — after years
        of cleaning — scrubbed sheen — shiny screen

kept from coming — undone — seams unraveled
    my body — my mind — held together now
        by thinnest thread — threatening to snap

at any moment — at any time — for any reason
    and let it all — before I can stop — fall apart
        into tiny pieces — sharp glass shards

I try not — to step on
cut open — my feet.

MATTHEW HAWK

DRIVE-IN MOVIE DURING A PANDEMIC

Midweek midsummer night at the drive-in,
only one other car ahead of us in line.
A gowned man in mask and gloves

scans our ticket with his handheld scanner,
directs us to tune our car radio and follow
signs straight ahead to our screen, where

we watch Jurassic Park and Jaws, two
different types of monster movies, which,
once so fearsome, now are almost laughable

with their low-tech recreation of our childhood
nightmares: dinosaur resurrections and shark
attacks. There are ten other cars sprawled out

at our showing, teens packed six to a car, families
crammed in the back of a pick-up truck, strewn
across an old air mattress. We tighten

our masks, roll up the car windows,
cringe as we see packs of stray youths
stroll up to the snack-shack maskless.

Even so, with our pillow and fleece-blanket,
we sit still in our crossover car, settle in
for the feature films, to be transported

to a bygone time when monsters
that went bump in the night
were the only worries we had.

MATTHEW HAWK

CONTRIBUTORS

Michael Alessi's work has recently appeared in *SmokeLong Quarterly, The Pinch, Passages North, Mid-American Review, The Cincinnati Review*, and other journals. He is the author of the prose chapbook *The Horribles* (Greying Ghost Press, 2019), and holds an MFA from Old Dominion University. A native of Virginia's Shenandoah Valley, he currently lives in Chicago.

Emma Aylor's poems have appeared or are forthcoming in *32 Poems, New Ohio Review, Pleiades, Colorado Review*, and the *Cincinnati Review*, among other journals, and she received *Shenandoah*'s 2020 Graybeal-Gowen Prize for Virginia Poets. She lives in Lubbock, Texas.

M. Christine Benner Dixon lives, writes, and grows things in Pittsburgh, Pennsylvania. Her writing has appeared in *HeartWood Literary Magazine, pacificREVIEW: A West Coast Arts Review Annual, Paperbark Literary Magazine, Tiny Seed Literary Journal, American Literary Realism*, and *DreamSeeker Magazine*.

Despy Boutris's writing has been published or is forthcoming in *Copper Nickel, American Poetry Review, The Gettysburg Review, Colorado Review, The Journal, Prairie Schooner*, and elsewhere. Currently, she teaches at the University of Houston and serves as Poetry Editor for *Gulf Coast*, Guest Editor for *Palette Poetry and Frontier*, and Editor-in-Chief of *The West Review*.

Monica Brashears is an MFA student at Syracuse University where she writes about the Black Appalachian experience, good food, womanhood. She has an upcoming publication with *Split Lip Magazine*, and she has just finished her first novel. Some of Monica's favorite things are as follows: fresh popcorn, full moons, and vanilla perfume.

Virginia Ottley Craghill's poems have appeared in *Think: A Journal of Poetry, Fiction, and Essays; Cumberland River Review; Kalliope; Atlanta Review; Gulf Coast; South Carolina Review;* and *The Chattahoochee Review*, among others. Her essays have been published in *The Best American Sports Writing 2018* and *The Sewanee Review*.

She currently lives in Sewanee, Tennessee, where she teaches in the English department at the University of the South.

Laura Demers has been published in the *North American Review* and *New Voices,* and she was nominated for the PEN/Robert J. Dau Short Story Prize for Emerging Writers in 2017. She was also a winner of *The Masters Review* 2018 Anthology Prize and a finalist for the Robert Day Award for Fiction. Her work appeared in *Granta*'s online magazine in 2020.

Martha Grace Duncan's memoirs have appeared in the *Gettysburg Review, Notre Dame Magazine, Passages North,* and *Tampa Review.* Five of her pieces have been chosen as "Notables" in the *Best American Essays* series, edited by Robert Atwan. Her memoir "A Perfect Start" won first prize in the Gail Wilson Kenna Creative Nonfiction Category in the 2018 Soul-Making Keats Literary Competition. An early version of her creative nonfiction piece, "What Not to Do When your Roommate is Murdered in Italy," won the 2014 Judith Siegel Pearson Award from Wayne State University. It was published in the *Harvard Journal of Law and Gender.*

Annie Frazier lives in North Carolina and received an MFA in fiction from Spalding University in 2017, where she served as Social Media Coordinator for the program and as a student editor for *The Louisville Review.* Her fiction and poetry has appeared in *Paper Darts, Hypertrophic Literary, Longleaf Review, Cabinet of Heed, Philosophical Idiot, CHEAP POP, Still: The Journal, Crack the Spine, apt magazine,* and *North Carolina Literary Review.*

Michael Garrigan writes and teaches along the Susquehanna River in Pennsylvania. He loves exploring the riverlands with a fly rod and believes that every watershed should have a Poet Laureate. He is the author of two poetry collections: *Robbing the Pillars* and *What I Know [How to Do].* His writing has appeared in *The Flyfish Journal, Split Rock Review,* and *The Hopper Magazine.* You can read more at www.mgarrigan.com.

Joseph Hardy is one of a handful of writers that live in Nashville, Tennessee, who does not play a musical instrument—although a friend once asked him to bring his harmonica on a camping trip so they could throw it in the fire. His work has been published in *Gyroscope Review, Inlandia, Penultimate Peanut, Structo*, and *the tiny journal*, among others.

Matthew Hawk is an MFA student at the University of Memphis, specializing in poetry. His work has been published in *Paradise in Limbo* literary magazine, the University of Chicago's Migration Stories project, and is forthcoming in *Rio Grande Review*. His chapbook, *Poems from the Heart*, was published by Desert Willow Press in 2018, and he was a semifinalist for *Iron Horse Literary Review*'s 2021 national poetry month contest.

DJ Hills is a writer and theatre artist from the Appalachian Mountains, currently living in Baltimore. Hills's writing appears or is forthcoming in *Arkansas Review, Cold Mountain Review, Lunch*, and elsewhere, and their plays have been produced in and around Baltimore City. When not writing, Hills reads fiction as the Co-Senior Fiction Editor at *jmww*. Find them online at www.dj-hills.com

Jessica Jewell is the author of three collections of poetry including *Slap Leather, Sisi and the Girl from Town*, and *Dust Runner*. She is also an editor of two collections: *Speak a Powerful Magic* and *I Hear the World Sing*. Jewell is currently the senior academic program director for the Wick Poetry Center at Kent State University, where she also earned her PhD in higher education administration and an MFA in poetry. Her poetry has appeared in *Cider Press Review, American Poetry Journal*, and *Nimrod* among others. Jewell lives in northeast Ohio with her wife and two gorgeous dogs.

Emily Masters lives in Columbia, South Carolina, where she works at Heathwood Hall Episcopal School. She serves as book reviews editor for *Appalachian Review* and associate fiction editor for *Still: The Journal*. She grew up on a farm in Monteagle, Tennessee, and graduated from Berea College in 2019. Her work has been published in *The Pikeville Review* and *Still: The Journal*.

Clay Matthews has published poetry in journals such as the *American Poetry Review, Blackbird, Kenyon Review, The Southern Review*, and elsewhere. His books are *Superfecta* (Ghost Road Press), *RUNOFF* (BlazeVox), *Pretty, Rooster* and *Shore* (both from Cooper

Dillon), and, most recently, *Four-Way Lug Wrench* (Main Street Rag Books). He currently lives in Elizabethtown, Kentucky, and teaches at Elizabethtown Community & Technical College.

Greta McDonough is the author of *Her Troublesome Boys: The Lucy Furman Story*. She writes a popular weekly column, "From this Place to That," for the *Owensboro Messenger-Inquirer*, and her writing has been featured in *Kentucky Living, Still: The Journal*, and *Appalachian Heritage*. Her photography has been exhibited at the Loyal Jones Appalachian Center at Berea College and featured in *Kudzu* and *Still: The Journal*.

Forrest Rapier has poetry forthcoming in *Dead Mule, Levee, Santa Clara Review,* and *Willawaw*. He has received fellowships from BOAAT, Looking Glass Falls, Sewanee Writers Conference, and has also held writing residencies at the University of Virginia and Brevard College. Former poetry editor for *Greensboro Review* and North Carolina Writers Network, he recently received his MFA from the University of North Carolina at Greensboro, where he works as a Library Programs Secretary for Guilford County.

Rosemary Royston, author of *Splitting the Soil* (Finishing Line Press, 2014), resides in northeast Georgia with her family. Her poetry and flash fiction has been published in journals such as *Split Rock Review, Southern Poetry Review, Appalachian Heritage, Poetry South, KUDZU, NANO Fiction,* and **82 Review*. She is an Assistant Professor of English at Young Harris College.

Misty Skaggs is a barefooted poet and a backwoods radical, born and raised in the Appalachian foothills where she still lives and writes. Her poetry collection *Planted by the Signs* is currently available from Ohio University Press.

Matt Vekakis is a gay poet & educator. He is grateful to have had poetry published in *Cathexis Northwest Press, Tule Review, Peregrine Journal, Waccamaw, Poached Hare, Gravitas,* and *Inklette Magazine,* with forthcoming publications in *Meat for Tea: The Valley Review and High Shelf Press*. He lives with his beau in the Tofu Valley of Western Massachusetts.